Veena Chopra's
Real Indian Cookery

VEENA CHOPRA'S REAL INDIAN COOKERY

foulsham

LONDON • NEW YORK • TORONTO • SYDNEY

foulsham

The Publishing House, Bennetts Close,
Cippenham, Berkshire SL1 5AP

ISBN 0-572-02507-6

Copyright © 1997 and 1999 Veena Chopra

Previously published under the title *The Real Indian Cookery Course*

Typeset by Westkey Ltd, Falmouth, Cornwall
Printed in Great Britain by
St Edmundsbury Press Ltd, Bury St Edmunds, Suffolk

DEDICATION

I dedicate this book to:

Late Mrs Jaswant Ahluwalia – my mother

Mr B. K. Ahluwalia – my father

Pritam – my husband

Sumeet – my son

Sajni – my daughter

ABOUT THE AUTHOR

Veena Chopra was born in the Punjab and grew up in a large household with many relations living together and several servants. Educated in Uttar Pradesh, she was an enthusiastic cook from childhood. In 1959 she received first prize for cooking in the Shajhanpur district. She trained as a teacher and is a post-graduate of Agra University, India.

She was married in 1970, after seeing her husband for only half an hour a few days before the wedding – as the marriage was arranged by her parents. She came to England with her husband, who is a physics teacher, four days after the marriage. They now live in Cambridge and have two children called Sumeet and Sajni.

Veena is a science co-ordinator at Blue Gate Fields Junior School and also teaches Indian cookery at many Cambridgeshire community colleges during the evening. She has given at times six-hour cookery demonstrations on Saturdays and has also been invited to do cookery demonstrations at various Women's Institute centres. Several of her cookery books have been published.

Veena sometimes gives demonstrations, with her two children, of traditional Indian dances at local cultural exhibitions and at various places in London. She enjoys playing the sitar.

CONTENTS

Step 5

Step 6

Step 7

Step 8

Step 9

CONTENTS

Step 15

Step 16

Step 17

Step 18

Step 19

Step 20

Step 21

Index

INTRODUCTION

This book has been written for all those who enjoy Indian food. Every part of India is different, its people and customs varied. Each area prides itself on a particularly special cuisine. Emigrant Indians have kept the flag of their native food's fragrance and flavour flying all over the world.

No one is a born cook. Practice, curiosity and need make one perfect. For instance, my mother had never cooked before her marriage. The first day after her wedding she was asked by Dadiji (my grandmother) to supervise and cook the afternoon meal. With a thumping heart and heavy feet she walked towards the kitchen. Tears were in her eyes. Ramu (the servant) noticed and closed the kitchen door. He suggested that he would cook the best meal he knew how on her behalf. The same day she wrote to her father to take her back for a month. She tried very hard to learn many dishes, not for the sake of cooking, but to win the heart of her darling and his family. She did so and made sure that her daughters – servants or no servants – must cook something special at least once a week so that they would not be in the same position when they married.

When we were little, we used to play a cooking game during the school holidays called 'Halkuliya' and the meaning we understood was 'work done together'. All the boys would go around the garden to pick up wood and bricks. Of course we couldn't borrow the wood or coal or use the kitchen fire otherwise it wouldn't be 'Halkuliya'. It was different to borrow flour, ghee, oil, potatoes, onions and utensils from mother and aunties. When we had collected everything, we would place three bricks to make a stove. My brothers would make the fire and go with our little sisters to hunt for more wood and large leaves. They would pick vegetables from our garden secretly so that the 'mali' (gardener) would not see them. The girls would start cooking. I had older girl cousins who would always make me sit and fry and it worked very nicely too because at seven years old I was happy to co-operate. I would do just as I was told (I wanted to be highly appreciated) but on the other hand I secretly passed some of the cooked food to my brothers and my little sisters who were working so hard in my opinion. At the end everyone would sit down and the food was served on large leaves. This was the most wonderful and satisfying food in our eyes. Pakora, puri, puri wallé aloo, mixed vegetables and kheer (rice pudding) were the dishes we most often attempted to do.

I am sure that this book is one of the most suitable books for everyone's kitchen shelf. The inception of this book dates back to 14 years ago when I started teaching cookery during the evenings at various centres in Cambridgeshire.

Week after week I heard my students say that they had just cooked the best dish of their lives, which was very encouraging and motivated me enough to put my oriental culinary expertise on to paper.

This book caters for all occasions: weddings, parties, daily meals, breakfast, tea, snacks, starters, drinks and chāts. It also contains popular mouth- watering dishes from all over India – North, South, East and West. I have included many popular breads, lentils, rice, meat, chicken, fish, vegetables, drinks, yoghurt, chutney and papadums. And since there is a vegetarian option for every day, the book can be used equally by both vegetarians and non-vegetarians. Simply choose the alternative recipe you prefer.

With practice the variety enables one to be in a position to host a banquet! A bonus point is that you'll be able to prepare things according to your own taste rather than what a restaurant offers you. Food cooked at home with freshly ground spices fills your dining-room with aroma, making you and your guests even more hungry.

A FEW POINTS TO REMEMBER

The most important thing is to read the recipe through completely at least once before actually starting to cook. Don't be put off by the large number of ingredients in each recipe. Most of these are standard spices which any Indian cook keeps in the cupboard. The following are a few handy hints while cooking:

1 BREAD:

When frying bread do not roll it in dry flour as it burns and discolours the cooking fat. Use oil instead of dry flour.

Do not throw bread in the middle of the hot oil pan, otherwise the hot oil will spit and splash. This can be dangerous. Slip a puri or bhutoora, katchori, bread roll, samosa etc. gently from the edge of the frying pan (skillet).

When rolling a chapati or paratha do not use too much dry flour because it burns quickly and gives a dark, burnt look to the bread.

2 BURNT DISH:

If you have burnt your dish, do not scrape the contents from the bottom. Put the top part of the dish into a clean saucepan and carry on cooking.

3 CAULIFLOWER:

A white-coloured cauliflower is always fresher, more tender and sweeter than a yellow one.

How to grate? Wash a whole cauliflower, take a knife and start cutting slices about 3 mm/⅛ in thick along the top. When you reach the stems then obviously grating with a grater will save you time.

4 COOKING TIME:

I cannot give exact cooking times because a lot depends on the quantity and quality (tenderness and age) of the food you want to cook.

5 CUMIN:

When added to hot oil cumin takes only 2 seconds to brown. Don't leave it any longer or it will burn.

To roast cumin: place a dry flat frying pan (skillet) on a medium heat, and add the cumin seeds. Stir until golden brown. Turn the heat off but keep on stirring. Leave to cool. Coarsely grind and keep in an airtight jar.

6 DOUGH:

It is difficult to explain what is soft, hard or stiff dough. Therefore I have given the quantity of water but at times you may have to adjust the quantity of the water slightly because the amount needed depends on the texture and moisture of the flour.

7 FROZEN FOOD:

Most of the cooked Indian food can be frozen unless stated otherwise in the recipe.

If frozen ingredients are used in any of the recipes then naturally the dish should not be re-frozen as some of its contents will have been frozen twice. (This does not apply for a short-term freezing.) If a recipe calls for frozen peas (for example) make and freeze the food without the peas and add them when reheating.

If any dish has been frozen, then sufficient time should be allowed for the food to be completely defrosted before reheating.

8 GARLIC AND GINGER:

Fresh garlic and ginger give the best flavour.
Always peel and wash before chopping or grinding.

9 GARAM MASALA:

Always sprinkle a little ground garam masala before
serving a dish so that it retains its pleasant aroma.
Whole garam masala (cloves, peppercorns, cinnamon
stick and black cardamom) retains its fragrance for a
long time, therefore I add them at the beginning
especially in a dish which contains sauce.

10 'HOTNESS' OF FOOD:

It is difficult to say how hot a dish is because it
depends on individual taste. One dish may be hot for
you but not for me or vice versa. The things which
make your dish hot are red and green chillies, so
increase or decrease the quantity of chillies according
to your taste. Food will be delicious even with just a
pinch of ground red chilli.

11 LEMON:

Always add lemon juice at the end once the lentils,
vegetables and meat are cooked and tender, otherwise
they will take longer to cook.

12 LENTILS:

In India lentils, or dal, have quite a runny consistency.
Thick and overcooked lentils lose their flavour.

13 LID:

Why close the lid on a saucepan while cooking?
  (a) The food cooks quicker.
  (b) The food retains its nutritional value.
  (c) The fragrance of the spices isn't lost.
  (d) The food is cooked in the steam.

14 MEASUREMENTS:

(a) All teaspoons are level.
(b) Onion size: small 50 g/2 oz, medium 100 g/ 4 oz, large 200 g/7 oz.

15 MICROWAVE OVEN:

The popularity of a microwave oven is increasing rapidly. It can be used to speed up defrosting. It is a marvellous gadget to reheat cooked food, and is especially good for rice dishes.

16 MILK:

Always rinse your saucepan before adding milk to boil. It will prevent milk sticking to the pan.

17 MUSTARD SEEDS:

When frying, cover the pan to avoid spitting.

18 OIL:

How to check that the oil is hot? Slip a little dough or batter or a thin slice of onion into the hot oil. If it sizzles and comes up at once the oil is hot and ready for cooking.

Keep leftover fried oil separate and use only for frying.

Never fry vegetables in oil in which you have fried fish, meat or chicken.

Always use fresh oil for dishes such as curries, rice etc.

19 ONION:

Always wash onions after peeling. If they make you cry soak them in cold water for a little while, or peel them in water, or after peeling cut in half and leave them aside for 10 minutes before you start chopping.

20 POPPY SEEDS:

They are often quite dirty so soak them in lukewarm water, drain, dry and grind them in a coffee grinder.

21 PRESSURE COOKER:

Using a pressure cooker can save time when cooking pulses. If using a pressure cooker, reduce the quantity of water stated in the recipe.

22 RICE:

To see if any water is left after cooking rice, tip the pan a little but do not stir. Place the pan back on a high heat and dry off any remaining water. Close the lid and leave for at least 5 minutes before serving.

Stir cooked rice gently with a fork before serving to make it light and fluffy.

Rice is very delicate when cooked; therefore it is best eaten immediately or it will become soggy.

23 SALT:

Indians take more salt through savoury yoghurt dishes and salty lemon squash etc., especially during the summer so that they can replace the salt which they have lost.

24 SPICES:

Grind your own spices such as coriander, cumin and garam masala, and store in a jar. This will give your recipes better flavour because:

(a) The spices are cleaned.
(b) They are fresh and whole spices store better.
(c) They are pure and not a mixture of other spices.
(d) They are full of fragrance.

25 TYMOL SEEDS:

Tymol seeds contain quite a lot of dirt. Therefore either clean them or soak and drain in a strainer before using.

26 UTENSILS:

For cooking, a saucepan or a frying pan (skillet) should be heavy. Whenever possible use stainless steel or enamel-ware saucepans because some of the ingredients, like tamarind, lemon, mango, cooking apples etc., contain acid which reacts with other metals.

27 VEGETARIAN RECIPES:

Vegetarian recipes are marked with a (V) symbol. These recipes do include dairy products such as milk and yoghurt.

28 WHOLE SPICES:

I like to add cloves, cinnamon, black pepper and black cardamoms to a curry while frying the onions. Whole spices retain their fragrance for longer periods than garam masala (after grinding the above spices one makes garam masala).

In India most people habitually put aside whole spices while eating their meal as if you chew whole spices by mistake they are very strong.

Therefore if you or your guests are not sure please leave the whole spices completely out of your dish and instead increase 2.5 ml/½ tsp garam masala in your recipe (for this purpose the whole spices have been asterisked* in the recipes).

MISCELLANEOUS

In this section, I will introduce you to some simple recipes which form the basis of many Indian dishes.

Nowadays you can buy Indian pastes and spices in every supermarket, but I am sure that you will find that mixing your own garam masala, sambar masala and roasting your own cumin will improve the flavour of your cooking. I think it is well worth the effort.

Ghee (a sort of cooking fat), paneer (Indian cheese) and yoghurt are all very easy to make. We use them all very often in Indian dishes and although, again, there are ready-made Western equivalents, I think you will want to try to achieve the most authentic Indian taste in you recipes. The method of cooking potatoes is very simple and time-saving.

Khoya and tamarind pulp are not so well known to Western cooks, but the more adventurous of you will want to try them too!

GARAM MASALA

This is an aromatic mixture of spices – the words mean 'hot spices'. The mixture is used sparingly and often put into a dish towards the end of the cooking time. It is also used as a garnish. Always make your own.

As I have said, there is no comparison between garam masala bought from a shop and that made at home. One can keep the home-made garam masala in an airtight container for at least three months without it losing its aroma.

INGREDIENTS:	METRIC	IMPERIAL	AMERICAN
Black cardamom, seeds only	25 g	1 oz	$\frac{1}{4}$ cup
Black peppercorns	25 g	1 oz	$\frac{1}{4}$ cup
Cloves	25 g	1 oz	$\frac{1}{4}$ cup
Cinnamon stick, broken into small pieces	25 g	1 oz	$\frac{1}{4}$ cup

Grind the above ingredients in a coffee grinder until they resemble the consistency of powder.

GHEE
Clarified butter

*S*ome families in northern India cook in ghee as opposed to oil. This is actually very fattening and many Indians nowadays use unsaturated fats. However ghee adds a delicious nutty flavour and a silky smoothness to recipes, and sweets especially taste a lot better if ghee is used.

INGREDIENTS:	METRIC	IMPERIAL	AMERICAN
Butter	500 g	1 lb 2 oz	$2^1/_4$ cups

Put the butter in a large saucepan and boil, stirring, until all the butter has melted. When the solids (whey) appear at the bottom and the clear part (ghee) is at the top, reduce the heat to low. Keep on stirring until it is light brown. Turn off the heat and keep stirring so that it does not boil over. Allow to cool slightly.

Put a muslin cloth over a container or jar and pour the contents of the saucepan into the cloth so that the ghee strains through into the container. Squeeze the remaining ghee from the muslin cloth and discard the contents of the cloth. Let the ghee cool down and then place the lid on the container and keep aside until required.

The cloth can be re-used after washing. Ghee can be kept for several months in an airtight container.

POTATOES BOILED IN THEIR JACKETS

Potatoes are inexpensive and are a staple ingredient of many dishes in Indian cooking. They are particularly good in dry, spicy vegetable side dishes. We usually like to boil potatoes in their jackets and then peel them.

INGREDIENTS:	METRIC	IMPERIAL	AMERICAN
Potatoes, washed	500 g	1 lb 2 oz	18 oz
Water	1.2 litres	2 pts	5 cups

Place the potatoes and the water in a large saucepan. Bring to the boil, reduce the heat to medium-low, close the lid, and cook for 20–25 minutes or until tender.

SAMBAR MASALA

This is a delicious paste for flavouring your recipes. You can keep sambar masala in an airtight jar for up to one month.

INGREDIENTS:	METRIC	IMPERIAL	AMERICAN
Coconut, desiccated, or fresh, grated	50 g	2 oz	¼ cup
Oil	15 ml	1 tbsp	1 tbsp
Whole coriander, cleaned	15 ml	1 tbsp	1 tbsp
Urid ki dhuli dal, cleaned	10 ml	2 tsp	2 tsp
Gram dal (split yellow peas), cleaned	10 ml	2 tsp	2 tsp
Fenugreek seeds	5 ml	1 tsp	1 tsp
Whole small dried red chillies	4	4	4

Heat the oil in a flat frying pan (skillet) on a medium-low heat and roast all the ingredients for 5 minutes or until light brown. Cool, then grind to a fine paste.

ROASTED CUMIN

When in a recipe I say ground cumin, it refers to roasted ground cumin. Roasting turns the seeds a few shades darker and brings out a wonderful aroma.

INGREDIENTS:	METRIC	IMPERIAL	AMERICAN
Cumin seeds	50 g	2 oz	1/4 cup

Heat a tawa or flat frying pan (skillet) (cast iron is best) on a medium-low heat. Place the cumin on it and keep on turning them over for 2 minutes or until brown. No fat is necessary. Cool and grind coarsely. Keep in an airtight jar. For best results use within a month of grinding.

PANEER
Indian cheese

Indian people like to make cheese at home. Indian cheese differs in taste from Western cheeses. One can fry paneer and it becomes softer and spongy when cooked.
  It can be used in both sweet and savoury dishes.

INGREDIENTS:	METRIC	IMPERIAL	AMERICAN
Milk (preferably gold top)	1.2 litres	2 pts	5 cups
Lemon juice	60 ml	4 tbsp	4 tbsp

Heat the milk in a heavy-bottomed saucepan. As it comes to the boil add the lemon juice (if needed add more) so that the milk separates into curd and pale yellow whey. Leave to set for 5 minutes. Do not throw away the whey because it contains minerals and can be used in curries instead of water to add extra taste.
  Line a strainer with a cloth, strain the milk and squeeze out the excess whey. Fold the cloth tightly around the paneer to form a square (about 10 cm/4 in square). Put on an upturned plate and place a heavy weight on top (such as a pan filled with water) to squeeze out any excess whey. Leave for about 4 hours to set. For most curries cut the paneer into small pieces (1 cm/½ in square) and fry them in a deep frying pan (skillet) on a medium heat until light golden brown or bake on a greased tray in a preheated oven at 200°C/400°F/gas mark 6 for 5 minutes. Do not fry or bake the paneer in a sweet recipe.

TAMARIND PULP

Tamarind trees are large and shady and that is why they are planted on the roadside. During the heat of summer the people, cows, goats etc. take shelter under them. We used to pick unripe tamarind on our way to school and eat them with salt and pepper. They are very sour (tart) and one cannot eat too many. When ripe, the stones are removed and after drying they are packed in bars. One can keep them for at least a year. Tamarind is full of iron.

INGREDIENTS:	METRIC	IMPERIAL	AMERICAN
Dried tamarind, soaked overnight or boiled in water for 15 minutes on a medium-low heat	100 g	4 oz	1 cup
	300 ml	½ pt	1¼ cups

Extract pulp from soaked or boiled and cooked tamarind by sieving, and throw away the seeds and the sticks etc. (The waste shouldn't exceed 15 ml/ 1 tbsp.) I use 300 ml/½ pt/1¼ cups cold water to extract the pulp and never add more than 45 ml/3 tbsp water at a time to sieve the pulp.

YOGHURT (HOME-MADE NATURAL YOGHURT)

To start making home-made natural yoghurt one needs thick natural live yoghurt from a supermarket. After that, use your home-made yoghurt as a culture. After a month, I restart the process.

INGREDIENTS:	METRIC	IMPERIAL	AMERICAN
Milk, boiled then cooled to lukewarm	600 ml	1 pt	2½ cups
Culture from a thick natural yoghurt, mixed with a little milk until smooth	15 ml	1 tbsp	1 tbsp

Place the milk in a saucepan or dish with tight lid. Mix the culture in the lukewarm milk, close the lid and leave it to set in an airing cupboard for 8 hours. When set (check it) keep it in the refrigerator for at least 3–4 hours before using.

KHOYA
Traditional method:

Khoya is made from milk. It is usually used to make Indian sweets, but is sometimes added to lavish curries.

INGREDIENTS:	METRIC	IMPERIAL	AMERICAN
Milk, rich cream	1.2 litres	2 pts	5 cups

Place the milk in a large heavy-bottomed saucepan and bring to the boil. Reduce the heat to medium-low and keep stirring until it solidifies. It will take about 2 hours.

Quick method:

Full cream milk powder	50 g	2 oz	½ cup
Ghee, melted	10 ml	2 tsp	2 tsp
Milk, lukewarm	30 ml	2 tbsp	2 tbsp

Combine all the above ingredients in a bowl, mix and form into a ball (like soft dough).

We start with a choice of main dishes and one of the most popular breads of India. You can try Undé Ki Sabji, an egg curry, or my delicious Whole Apple Curry, both very much in my mother's style of cooking. If you like, you can serve rice with the meal. Try also to prepare Coconut and Chocolate Barfi, a delicious Indian sweet to finish your meal.

✳ Undé Ki Sabji

EGG CURRY, MY MOTHER'S STYLE

SERVES 4–6

My mother created this hearty dish. It was one of the dishes I cooked for my prize-winning entry in the Shajhanpur district competition. It is medium-hot. (Undé means egg.)

1ST STAGE: MAKING THE PASTE:

INGREDIENTS:	METRIC	IMPERIAL	AMERICAN
Oil or ghee	150 ml	5 fl oz	$^2/_3$ cup
Cumin seeds	5 ml	1 tsp	1 tsp
Medium onion, finely chopped	1	1	1
*Cloves	4	4	4
*Peppercorns	4	4	4
*Cinnamon stick	2.5 cm	1 in	1 in
*Black cardamom	1	1	1
Bay leaves	4	4	4

2ND STAGE: FOR THE BLENDED PASTE:

Large garlic cloves, coarsely chopped	4	4	4
Medium onions, coarsely chopped	3	3	3
Fresh ginger, coarsely chopped	2.5 cm	1 in	1 in

Combine the garlic, onions and ginger in a blender and blend with 30 ml/2 tbsp water to make a smooth paste.

Poppy seeds, finely ground	25 g	1 oz	$^1/_4$ cup
Coconut, desiccated or fresh, ground very finely in a grinder	75 g	3 oz	$^3/_4$ cup
Ground coriander/cilantro	10 ml	2 tsp	2 tsp
Ground turmeric	2.5 ml	$^1/_2$ tsp	$^1/_2$ tsp

UNDÉ KI SABJI

Ground red chilli	2.5 ml	½ tsp	½ tsp
Garam masala	5 ml	1 tsp	1 tsp
Salt to taste			
Tomatoes, tinned	400 g	14 oz	1¾ cups
Lemon juice	15 ml	1 tbsp	1 tbsp
Eggs, hard-boiled (hard-cooked), shelled and cut into halves lengthwise	6	6	6

TO GARNISH:

Garam masala	2.5 ml	½ tsp	½ tsp
Green coriander/cilantro leaves, chopped	15 ml	1 tbsp	1 tbsp
Small green chilli, chopped (optional)	1	1	1

COOKING TIME: 1 HOUR

1 Heat the oil or ghee in a large heavy-bottomed saucepan and brown the cumin seeds. Add the chopped onion, the whole spices and fry gently until golden brown on medium heat.

2 Stir in the blended paste and fry for 5 minutes.

3 Put in the ground poppy seeds and fry for 2 minutes.

4 Then add the ground coconut and fry everything for a further few minutes until golden brown.

5 Stir in the ground spices (coriander, turmeric, red chilli, garam masala), salt and tomatoes. Fry until all the liquid has been absorbed and the oil appears on the surface of the mixture.

6 Pour in 45 ml/3 tbsp water and fry until all the water is absorbed. Repeat this twice so that the spices can mature.

7 Add 250 ml/8 fl oz/1 cup water and the lemon juice. Bring to boil, reduce the heat to low, and simmer for 3 minutes.

GARNISH SUGGESTIONS:

Pour the hot sauce in a serving dish. Place the eggs on the top and sprinkle over the garnish before serving

SERVING SUGGESTION:

Serve hot with rice, puri, dahi bara, beans and potato curry; if you are serving with rice, pour the sauce over the rice, place the eggs on top and sprinkle over the garnish.

❋
WHOLE
APPLE CURRY

MY MOTHER'S STYLE

SERVES: 4–6

This satisfying dish was also created by my mother. It is medium-hot.

1ST STAGE: MAKING THE PASTE

INGREDIENTS:	METRIC	IMPERIAL	AMERICAN
Large garlic cloves, coarsely chopped	4	4	4
Medium onions, coarsely chopped	3	3	3
Fresh ginger, coarsely chopped	2.5 cm	1 in	1 in

Combine the garlic, onions and ginger and blend with 60 ml/4 tbsp water to make a smooth paste.

Oil or ghee	150 ml	5 fl oz	$^2/_3$ cup
Cumin seeds	5 ml	1 tsp	1 tsp
Medium onion, finely chopped	1	1	1
*Cloves	4	4	4
*Peppercorns	4	4	4
*Cinnamon stick	2.5 cm	1 in	1 in
*Black cardamom	1	1	1
Bay leaves	4	4	4
Poppy seeds, finely ground	25 g	1 oz	$^1/_4$ cup
Coconut, desiccated or fresh, ground very finely in a grinder	75 g	3 oz	$^3/_4$ cup
Ground coriander/cilantro	10 ml	2 tsp	2 tsp
Ground turmeric	2.5 ml	$^1/_2$ tsp	$^1/_2$ tsp
Ground red chilli	2.5 ml	$^1/_2$ tsp	$^1/_2$ tsp
Garam masala	5 ml	1 tsp	1 tsp
Salt to taste			
Tomatoes, tinned	400 g	14 oz	$1^3/_4$ cups

Medium whole apples, pips and core removed and the apple pricked all over with a fork	8	8	8
Lemon juice	15 ml	1 tbsp	1 tbsp

TO GARNISH:

Garam masala	2.5 ml	½ tsp	½ tsp
Green coriander/cilantro leaves, chopped	15 ml	1 tbsp	1 tbsp
Small green chilli, chopped (optional)	1	1	1

COOKING TIME: 1 HOUR

1 Heat the oil in a large heavy-bottomed saucepan and brown the cumin seeds. Add the chopped onion, the whole spices and fry gently until golden brown on medium heat.

2 Stir in the blended paste and fry for 5 minutes.

3 Put in the ground poppy seeds and fry for 2 minutes.

4 Then add the ground coconut and fry everything for a further few minutes until golden brown.

5 Stir in the ground spices (coriander, turmeric, red chilli, garam masala), salt and tomatoes. Fry until all the liquid has been absorbed and the oil appears on the surface of the mixture.

6 Pour in 45 ml/3 tbsp water and fry until all the water is absorbed. Repeat this twice so that the spices can mature in the sauce.

7 Place the apples in a pan with 150 ml/¼ pt/½ cup water and cook until all the liquid has been absorbed, covering the pan and stirring it gently from time to time.

8 Add 250 ml/8 fl oz 1 cup water and the lemon juice. Bring to the boil, reduce the heat to low, close the lid and simmer for 3 minutes.

GARNISH SUGGESTION:

Pour the hot sauce in a serving dish. Place the whole apples on the top and sprinkle over the garnish before serving.

SERVING SUGGESTION:

Serve hot with rice, puri and rayta or dahi bara.

PURI

MAKES: 18

Puri is probably the most popular bread and is used all over India. It is easy, quick to make and suitable for serving to guests. An average adult will consume about 4 puris.

MAKING THE DOUGH:

INGREDIENTS:	METRIC	IMPERIAL	AMERICAN
Brown chapati flour	500 g	1 lb 2 oz	5 cups
Oil	30 ml	2 tbsp	2 tbsp
Large pinch of salt			
Water, lukewarm	250 ml	8 fl oz	1 cup

1 Place the flour in a bowl.

2 Rub in the oil and salt thoroughly.

3 Knead the dough with the warm water for 2–5 minutes or until the dough is springy and satiny.

4 Cover and leave for 30 minutes.

FRYING THE PURI:

COOKING TIME: 30 MINUTES

1 Pour enough oil into your frying pan (skillet) to fill to three-quarters full.

2 Heat the oil on medium heat. While the oil is heating, divide the dough into 18 equal portions.

3 Take a portion of dough and roll it into a ball on the palm of your hands. Flatten it, place a few drops of oil on the rolling board and roll it into a thin (5 mm/¼ in) round with a rolling pin.

4 Slip a puri into the hot oil from the edge of the pan. Gently but swiftly press the puri all over with a slotted spoon and it will rise like a balloon.

5 Fry both sides until golden brown. I roll another puri while one is frying.

SERVING SUGGESTION:

Serve hot with a meal. Puri goes superbly with any sort of vegetable, lentil or yoghurt dish.

COCONUT AND CHOCOLATE BARFI

MAKES: 24

*T*his sweet is very popular with coconut-lovers and children. The yellow and brown colours look very attractive and stimulate the appetite.

INGREDIENTS:	METRIC	IMPERIAL	AMERICAN
Full cream milk powder	125 g	4³/₄ oz	1¹/₂ cups
Double (heavy) cream, whisked to thicken	150 ml	¹/₄ pt	²/₃ cup
Ghee	5 ml	1 tsp	1 tsp
Ground green cardamom	1.5 ml	¹/₄ tsp	¹/₄ tsp

Place the above ingredients in a bowl. Mix thoroughly and set to one side.

Coconut, desiccated	75 g	3 oz	¹/₃ cup
Ghee	10 ml	2 tsp	2 tsp
Sugar	75 g	3 oz	¹/₃ cup
Ground green cardamom	5 ml	1 tsp	1 tsp
Colouring, yellow	2.5 ml	¹/₂ tsp	¹/₂ tsp
Milk chocolate (for optional cake covering)	100 g	4 oz	¹/₂ cup

COOKING TIME: 20 MINUTES

1 Place the coconut and the ghee in a saucepan and fry it light brown on a low heat.

2 Add the milk powder mixture, sugar, green cardamom and colouring. Cook this on medium-low heat.

3 Stir thoroughly until the mixture thickens sufficiently to set. This is normally 5 minutes after the mixture seems to come away from the pan. The mixture should hold together and be non-sticky.

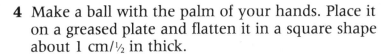

4 Make a ball with the palm of your hands. Place it on a greased plate and flatten it in a square shape about 1 cm/½ in thick.

5 Break the milk chocolate into small pieces in a small bowl and melt over a saucepan containing simmering water.

6 Pour the milk chocolate over the coconut barfi.

7 Leave to set for 3–4 hours.

8 Cut into square or diamond shapes (with sides about 3 cm/1¼ in long).

SERVING SUGGESTION:

Serve cold after a meal or at tea with samosa, pakora, madhi or dalmod etc.

Step 2 includes Sindhi-style Meat, a meat dish from the west of India, and a spinach and Indian cheese dish from the north. I am also going to introduce you to the most simple bread eaten daily in India. This is Chapati. And since no Indian meal is complete with a yoghurt side dish you will also learn how to make a simple and delicious rayta.

✳ SINDHI-STYLE MEAT

SERVES: 4

This is a medium-hot dish with the exotic flavour of fenugreek leaves.

INGREDIENTS:	METRIC	IMPERIAL	AMERICAN
Oil or ghee	75 ml	5 tbsp	5 tbsp
Medium onions, finely chopped	2	2	2
Bay leaves	2	2	2
Large garlic cloves, crushed	5	5	5
Fresh ginger, finely chopped	4 cm	1½ in	1½ in
Mutton or lamb, boned, cut into 2.5 cm/1 in pieces, fat trimmed off and washed	500 g	1 lb 2 oz	18 oz
Ground coriander/cilantro	10 ml	2 tsp	2 tsp
Garam masala	5 ml	1 tsp	1 tsp
Ground turmeric	2.5 ml	½ tsp	½ tsp
Ground red chilli	2.5 ml	½ tsp	½ tsp
Salt to taste			
Tomatoes, tinned	400 g	14 oz	1¾ cups
Fenugreek leaves, chopped	45 ml	3 tbsp	3 tbsp
OR dried methi leaves	15 ml	1 tbsp	1 tbsp
Natural yoghurt	150 ml	¼ pt	⅔ cup
Garam masala	2.5 ml	½ tsp	½ tsp

TO GARNISH:

	METRIC	IMPERIAL	AMERICAN
Garam masala	2.5 ml	½ tsp	½ tsp
Green coriander/cilantro leaves, chopped	15 ml	1 tbsp	1 tbsp
Small green chilli, chopped	1	1	1

COOKING TIME: 1 HOUR

1 Heat the oil or ghee in a heavy-bottomed saucepan on a medium heat and fry the chopped onion until gold.

STEP
2

2 Add the bay leaves, garlic and ginger, and fry until golden brown.

3 Add the meat pieces and fry until light brown.

4 Stir in the coriander, garam masala, turmeric, red chilli, salt and tomatoes, and cook until all the liquid has been absorbed.

5 Add the fenugreek leaves and yoghurt and cook until oil appears at the top.

6 Pour in 150 ml/½ pt/⅔ cup water. Reduce the heat to low, close the lid and simmer until the meat is tender.

7 Sprinkle over the garnish before serving.

SERVING SUGGESTION:

Serve hot with plain rice, chapati and cauliflower. To serve with rice, add a little more water to give you a runnier sauce.

✻
PALAK PANEER

SPINACH AND INDIAN CHEESE

SERVES: 6

This is a superb dish especially for vegetarians. It has a very high food value and is full of protein, iron and many minerals. It is a delicious party dish but I like to cook it at least once a week and my family love it. You will find this dish to be medium-hot.

INGREDIENTS:	METRIC	IMPERIAL	AMERICAN
Oil or ghee	90 ml	6 tbsp	6 tbsp
Medium onions, finely chopped	2	2	2
Large garlic cloves, crushed	4	4	4
Fresh ginger, finely chopped	2.5 cm	1 in	1 in
Ground coriander/cilantro	10 ml	2 tsp	2 tsp
Garam masala	10 ml	2 tsp	2 tsp
Ground roasted cumin	5 ml	1 tsp	1 tsp
Ground red chilli	2.5 ml	½ tsp	½ tsp
Ground turmeric	2.5 ml	½ tsp	½ tsp
Salt to taste			
Tomatoes, tinned	400 g	14 oz	1¾ cups
Spinach, finely chopped frozen, thawed	450 g	1 lb	16 oz
Green chilli, chopped	1	1	1
Paneer (see page 23), cut into 1 cm/½ in squares and either fried in a deep frying pan or baked on a greased tray at 200°C/400°F/gas mark 6 for 5 minutes	3.6 litres	6 pts	15 cups

COOKING TIME: 25 MINUTES

1 Heat the oil or ghee in a heavy-bottomed saucepan. Add the onions, garlic and ginger and fry until golden brown.

2 Stir in the ground spices, salt and the tomatoes and cook until the ghee/oil appears on the surface of the mixture.

3 Then add the spinach, green chilli and the paneer pieces.

4 Cover the saucepan and leave to simmer on medium-low heat for a further 5–7 minutes or until the paneer is soft and spongy (if necessary add a little water) and the spinach liquid has been absorbed.

SERVING SUGGESTION:

Serve hot with any bread, rice, lentils and rayta.

CHAPATI

MAKES: 9

Chapati is also very commonly known as roti or phulka. Chapati is a fairly easy bread to cook and digest, and therefore it is eaten daily in India. It can be made from plain white flour or brown chapati flour. (If you cannot get hold of the latter, mix equal quantities of wholemeal and white flour.)

INGREDIENTS:	METRIC	IMPERIAL	AMERICAN
Chapati flour	250 g	9 oz	1 cup
Water, lukewarm	150 ml	¼ pt	⅔ cup
Butter or ghee to spread			

MAKING THE DOUGH:

1 Keep aside a handful of flour for rolling-out. Place the chapati flour in a bowl.

2 Mix in the water to make a soft dough. Knead for 2 minutes or until the dough is springy and satiny. Cover and leave aside for 10 minutes.

MAKING THE CHAPATI:

COOKING TIME: 25 MINUTES

1 Divide the dough into 9 equal portions.

2 Take a portion of dough and roll it into a ball in the palm of your hands. Flatten, and dust in dry flour.

3 Roll out on a rolling board into a thin round circle.

4 Heat a flat frying pan (skillet) on medium heat. Place the chapati on it and cook for about 1 minute (you should see a slight colour change over the whole chapati), turn over and lightly cook on the other side for about 1 minute, making sure all the edges are cooked.

5 Turn again and press the chapati gently with a clean cloth and it will rise like a balloon (it will take 30–45 seconds). I roll my next chapati while one is cooking. Spread one face of the cooked chapati with butter or ghee (5 ml/1 tsp).

SERVING SUGGESTION:

Serve hot with all sorts of curries.

TOMATO, CUCUMBER AND ONION RAYTA

SERVES: 4–6

*T*his is one of the most popular yoghurt dishes in India, and is incredibly easy and quick to make. This rayta goes excellently with most Indian dishes.

PREPARING THE RAYTA:

INGREDIENTS:	METRIC	IMPERIAL	AMERICAN
Natural yoghurt, chilled and whisked until smooth	500 ml	17 fl oz	2¼ cups
Salt to taste			
Ground roasted cumin	2.5 ml	½ tsp	½ tsp
Tomatoes, washed and cut into 1.2 cm/½ in pieces	150 g	5 oz	1¼ cups
Small onion, finely chopped	1	1	1
Cucumber, washed and cut into 1.2 cm/½ in pieces	½	½	½

TO GARNISH:

	METRIC	IMPERIAL	AMERICAN
Ground roasted cumin	2.5 ml	½ tsp	½ tsp
Green coriander/cilantro leaves, chopped	15 ml	1 tbsp	1 tbsp
Small green chilli, chopped	1	1	1

PREPARATION TIME: 10 MINUTES

1 Place the whisked yoghurt in a deep bowl. Mix in the salt and ground cumin.

2 A few minutes before you want to eat, add the tomatoes, onion, and cucumber pieces.

3 Mix them thoroughly.

4 Sprinkle over the garnish before serving.

SERVING SUGGESTION:

Serve chilled with a meal.

STEP 3

In this section, one of the most popular starters/snacks – Vegetable Samosas with Tamarind Chutney – is awaiting you. Samosas are consumed all over the world. Even the supermarkets could not resist the temptation of selling them. If you follow the recipe carefully you will be able to produce the most delicious fresh and crispy samosas. Not only that, but the money you save by making them yourself will be enough to treat yourself to another of my cookery books! You can also learn how to make another popular sweet called Jalebi.

VEGETABLE SAMOSAS

MAKES: 16

Vegetable samosas are one of the most delicious and popular snacks, among both vegetarians and non-vegetarians. The dough can be prepared by two methods, and both are given below.

PREPARING THE DOUGH: METHOD 1

INGREDIENTS:	METRIC	IMPERIAL	AMERICAN
Plain/all-purpose flour, sifted	200 g	7 oz	1¾ cups
Lemon juice	5 ml	1 tsp	1 tsp
Small pinch of salt			
Water, lukewarm	75 ml	5 tbsp	5 tbsp

Place 150 g/5 oz/1¼ cups flour in a bowl. Mix in the lemon juice and the salt. Knead the dough with the water for 5 minutes or until the dough is springy and satiny. Cover and set on one side for 10 minutes.

METHOD 2

Plain/all-purpose flour, sifted	150 g	5 oz	1¼ cups
Oil	5 ml	1 tsp	1 tsp
Small pinch of salt			
Water, lukewarm	75 ml	5 tbsp	5 tbsp

Place the sifted flour in a bowl. Mix in the oil and the salt. Knead the dough with the water for 5 minutes or until the dough is springy and satiny. Cover and set on one side for 10 minutes.

PREPARING THE FILLING:

Oil	45 ml	3 tbsp	3 tbsp
Cumin seeds	5 ml	1 tsp	1 tsp
Potatoes, boiled in jackets, peeled then diced	500 g	1 lb 2 oz	4½ cups
Garam masala	5 ml	1 tsp	1 tsp

Ground roasted cumin	5 ml	1 tsp	1 tsp
Ground ginger	2.5 ml	½ tsp	½ tsp
Ground red chilli	2.5 ml	½ tsp	½ tsp
Ground turmeric	2.5 ml	½ tsp	½ tsp
Salt to taste			
Peas, frozen, or fresh, shelled	250 g	9 oz	2¼ cups
Lemon juice	30 ml	2 tbsp	2 tbsp
Sugar	15 ml	1 tbsp	1 tbsp
Green coriander/cilantro leaves, chopped	10 ml	2 tsp	2 tsp
Small green chilli, chopped	1	1	1
Oil for frying and smearing			

COOKING TIME: 20 MINUTES

1 Heat the oil in a deep frying pan (skillet) on medium heat and brown the cumin seeds.

2 Add the potato pieces and fry for 10 minutes or until light golden brown.

3 Stir in the ground spices, salt and the frozen peas and cook until tender.

4 Mix in the lemon juice and the sugar and cook for 2 minutes.

5 Turn the heat off, add the coriander leaves and the green chilli and mix them well.

6 Leave to cool on one side and divide into 16 equal portions.

PREPARING THE PASTRY: METHOD 1

1 Make a runny batter using 15 ml/1 tbsp flour and 15–30 ml/1–2 tbsp water and set to one side.

2 Divide the dough into 8 equal portions.

3 Roll each piece into a ball in the palm of your hands.

4 Dust them in flour, then roll them into small circles.

5 Sprinkle some flour on the rolling board, place a circle on the board, smear the top with oil, making sure you smear the edges, sprinkle some flour on it and place another circle on top. Repeat this so that 4 circles lie on top of each other.

6 Sprinkle some flour on top, then roll the whole thing out thinly.

7 Heat a flat frying pan (skillet) on medium heat. Reduce to low heat and place the rolled circles on it. Bake for 10–20 seconds or until dry, turn over and remove the first layer, immediately turn over again and remove the second layer, turn over and remove the third and fourth layers.

8 Place them on a cooling tray and cover with a tea towel.

9 Repeat with the rest of the dough.

10 Cut the rounds in half.

11 Take one half and, by bringing the corners towards each other, let the flat edge meet and overlap in the centre, forming a cone shape.

12 Brush one side of the overlap with batter and stick down firmly.

13 Fill the cone with potato mixture.

14 Brush the edges with batter and firmly seal the cone.

At this stage the samosas can be frozen and then freshly deep fried when one wants to serve. With practice this method is quicker and the pastry is very fine and crisp.

METHOD 2

1 Divide the dough into 8 equal portions.

2 Take a portion of dough and roll it into a ball in the palm of your hand, flatten it, place a few drops of oil on the rolling board and thinly roll into a large circle.

3 Cut the circle in half.

4 Make a cone, fill and seal as in method 1 except this time sealing with water.

5 Pinch the arched edge with your fingers to give an attractive pattern.

6 These should be fried first before freezing and reheated under a grill.

FRYING THE SAMOSAS:

FRYING TIME: 20 MINUTES

Heat the oil in a deep frying pan (skillet) on medium heat. Gently slip 5 or 6 samosas into the hot oil, reduce heat to medium-low and fry until crispy light golden brown on all sides (do not fry too quickly).

SERVING SUGGESTION:

Serve hot with tamarind chutney, gulab jamun or rasgulla, a sweet dish from Bengal, at tea.

TAMARIND CHUTNEY

FILLS: 450 G/1 LB JAM JAR

Tamarind chutney is not only delicious, but an excellent source of iron and other minerals. It will keep for a long time in an airtight container if a clean dry spoon is used to take it out. The chutney is acidic, so while cooking and eating use a wooden or stainless steel spoon. You will find the chutney to be quite hot.

INGREDIENTS:	METRIC	IMPERIAL	AMERICAN
Dried tamarind, soaked overnight	100 g	4 oz	1 cup
°Water	300 ml	$\frac{1}{2}$ pt	$1\frac{1}{4}$ cups
Sugar	250 g	9 oz	$2\frac{1}{4}$ cups
Garam masala	5 ml	1 tsp	1 tsp
Ground roasted cumin	5 ml	1 tsp	1 tsp
Ground red chilli	2.5 ml	$\frac{1}{2}$ tsp	$\frac{1}{2}$ tsp
Salt (or black salt) to taste			
Raisins	50 g	2 oz	$\frac{1}{3}$ cup
Dried dates, pitted and finely sliced	5	5	5

°If you are unable to soak your tamarind overnight, boil it in the water for 15 minutes on low heat.

COOKING TIME: 15 MINUTES

1 Extract the pulp from soaked/boiled tamarind by sieving it thoroughly. Throw away the seeds and the sticks (the waste should not exceed 15 ml/ 1 tbsp). I use 300 ml/½ pt/1¼ cups cold water to extract the pulp, never adding more than 50–60 ml/3–4 tbsp at a time to sieve the pulp.

2 Place the pulp on high heat with the sugar and all the ground spices. Bring to the boil and reduce the heat to medium-low and cook for 10 minutes.

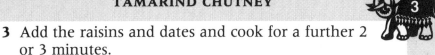

3 Add the raisins and dates and cook for a further 2 or 3 minutes.

4 Let the chutney cool down (open to the air), then put it into clean jars.

SERVING SUGGESTION:

Serve cold with a main meal or with samosa, pakora, kebab, bread rolls etc. at tea-time.

JALEBI

SERVES: 4–6

Jalebi is a delightful Indian sweet. Every Sunday we used to have it for breakfast. Some people like to eat jalebi with milk and yoghurt.

MAKING THE BATTER:

INGREDIENTS:	METRIC	IMPERIAL	AMERICAN
Dried yeast	5 ml	1 tsp	1 tsp
Water, lukewarm	45 ml	3 tbsp	3 tbsp

Place the yeast and water into a small bowl. Beat with a fork, cover and leave in a warm place for 30 minutes. It should rise and foam up.

Plain/all-purpose flour, sifted	100 g	4 oz	1 cup
Lemon juice	5 ml	1 tsp	1 tsp
Water, lukewarm	100 ml	$3^{1}/_2$ fl oz	$6^{1}/_2$ tbsp

1 Mix the sifted flour and the lemon juice into the risen yeast.

2 Gradually add the water to make a smooth batter.

3 Cover and leave for 1 hour; it should double in size.

PREPARING THE SYRUP:

Water	250 ml	8 fl oz	1 cup
Sugar	150 g	5 oz	$^{2}/_3$ cup
Colouring, yellow	5 ml	1 tsp	1 tsp

1 Place the water and the sugar in a saucepan.

2 Bring to the boil on medium heat

3 Stir in the colour and reduce the heat to very low and let it simmer while you make the jalebi.

COOKING TIME: 45 MINUTES

1 Heat a mixture of ghee and oil (equal quantities) in a deep frying pan (skillet) on medium heat.

2 Mix the batter with a fork.

3 I use an empty, cleaned and dried washing-up liquid bottle for this stage, but one can use an icing bag with a medium nozzle. Take the lid or cap off the bottle. Place a funnel on the bottle and pour in the batter. Put the cap back on.

4 Hold the bottle upside down, 15 cm/6 in above the hot fat, gently press the bottle but swiftly move your hand to form the batter into coiled circles or spirals in the hot fat.

5 Fry 4 or 5 jalebi together until golden brown on both sides.

6 Take them out with a slotted spoon, dip in the hot syrup and let them soak for 30 seconds, turn them over and let them soak for a further 15 seconds. Drain and remove all the jalebi from the syrup and put them on a cooling tray.

7 Repeat until all the batter is used.

SERVING SUGGESTION:

Serve hot at breakfast, after a meal or as a sweet snack. The jalebi can be reheated under a grill.

STEP 4

Let me take you to the north of India. Have a taste of Khatéwalé Kabuli Chunna (chickpeas), Dum Aloo (potatoes), Dahi Bara (yoghurt) and Bhutoora (bread). These mouth-watering dishes can convert anyone to be a fan of Indian food. They are popular all over India and are suitable for all occasions.

Also awaiting you is Prawn Pulao prepared in an East Indian (Bengal) style.

KHATÉWALÉ KABULI CHUNNA

CHICKPEAS NORTH INDIAN STYLE

SERVES 4–6

This is a very popular dish from the Punjab and it is suitable for parties and important ceremonies. You will find this dish to be medium-hot.

INGREDIENTS:	METRIC	IMPERIAL	AMERICAN
Chickpeas/garbanzos, soaked overnight and cleaned	500 g	1 lb 2 oz	$4^1/_2$ cups
Gram dal, cleaned	50 g	2 oz	$^1/_4$ cup
Bicarbonate of soda/baking soda	2.5 ml	$^1/_2$ tsp	$^1/_2$ tsp
Salt to taste			
Water	2.75 litres	5 pts	12 cups
Oil or ghee	75 ml	5 tbsp	5 tbsp
Cumin seeds	5 ml	1 tsp	1 tsp
Large garlic cloves, crushed	3	3	3
Fresh ginger, chopped	2.5 cm	1 in	1 in
Large onion, finely chopped	1	1	1
Ground coriander/cilantro	10 ml	2 tsp	2 tsp
Ground cumin	5 ml	1 tsp	1 tsp
Garam masala	5 ml	1 tsp	1 tsp
Ground turmeric	2.5 ml	$^1/_2$ tsp	$^1/_2$ tsp
Ground red chilli	2.5 ml	$^1/_2$ tsp	$^1/_2$ tsp
Tomatoes, tinned	400 g	14 oz	$1^3/_4$ cups
Tamarind, soaked overnight and pulp extracted (see page 24)	50 g	2 oz	2 oz

TO GARNISH:

Green coriander leaves, chopped	30 ml	2 tbsp	2 tbsp
Small green chilli, chopped	1	1	1
Garam masala	2.5 ml	1 tsp	1 tsp

COOKING TIME: 1 HOUR 40 MINUTES

1 Place the chickpeas, gram dal, bicarbonate of soda, salt and water in a large pan. If you do not have a pan large enough, add water gradually throughout cooking time. Bring to the boil, skim off any scum and simmer over medium heat for 1 hour 20 minutes until the chickpeas are tender. Drain.

2 Meanwhile, heat the oil or ghee in a heavy-based pan and fry the cumin seeds until lightly browned.

3 Add the garlic, ginger and onion and fry over medium heat until golden brown.

4 Stir in the ground spices and the tomatoes and cook until all the water has been absorbed and the oil appears on the top of the mixture.

5 Add the tamarind pulp and cook until all the liquid has been absorbed.

6 Stir in the cooked chickpeas and simmer over medium heat for a further 20 minutes until the mixture thickens.

7 Sprinkle over the garnish ingredients.

SERVING SUGGESTION:

Serve hot with bhutoora or naan, tamarind chutney, dahi bara, matar paneer and potato curry. A salad of finely chopped onion and tomato can be sprinkled over the top.

❋
PRAWN PULAO

SERVES 4–6

This delicious combination of layers of rice and prawns originates from Bengal. It is a delicate dish and best eaten the moment it is prepared. You will find it to be medium-hot.

PREPARING THE RICE:

INGREDIENTS:	METRIC	IMPERIAL	AMERICAN
Ghee	75 ml	5 tbsp	5 tbsp
Cumin seeds	5 ml	1 tsp	1 tsp
*Cloves	4	4	4
*Peppercorns	4	4	4
Bay leaves	2	2	2
*Cardamom	1	1	1
*Cinnamon stick	1.2 cm	½ in	½ in
Rice (patna or basmati), cleaned, washed and drained	225 g	8 oz	1 cup
Garam masala	2.5 ml	½ tsp	½ tsp
Salt to taste			
Water	400 ml	14 fl oz	2 cups

COOKING TIME: 25 MINUTES

1 Heat the ghee in a large heavy-bottomed saucepan, brown the cumin seeds and then add the whole spices and the rice. Stir the mixture for 2 minutes until it no longer sticks.

2 Add the garam masala, salt and water; bring to boil on high heat.

3 Reduce the heat to minimum. Cover the pan and simmer for 15 minutes. (Remember not to stir it or lift the lid before the end of the cooking time.)

PREPARING THE PRAWNS:

Oil	75 ml	5 tbsp	5 tbsp
Large garlic cloves, crushed	3	3	3

PRAWN PULAO

Medium onion, thinly sliced	1	1	1
Fresh ginger, chopped	2.5 cm	1 in	1 in
Ground coriander/cilantro	5 ml	1 tsp	1 tsp
Ground roasted cumin	5 ml	1 tsp	1 tsp
Ground red chilli	2.5 ml	½ tsp	½ tsp
Ground turmeric	2.5 ml	½ tsp	½ tsp
Tomatoes, tinned	230 g	8 oz	1 cup
Natural yoghurt	150 ml	¼ pt	⅔ cup
Coconut, desiccated, or fresh, grated	50 g	2 oz	¼ cup
Salt to taste			
Large peeled prawns (shrimp), fresh or frozen	250 g	9 oz	2¼ cups
Milk	50 ml	2 fl oz	3½ tbsp

TO GARNISH:

Green coriander/cilantro leaves, chopped	15 ml	1 tbsp	1 tbsp
Garam masala	5 ml	1 tsp	1 tsp
Small green chilli, chopped	1	1	1

COOKING TIME: 30 MINUTES

1 Prepare the prawns while the rice is cooking.

2 Heat the oil in a frying pan (skillet). Add the garlic, onion and ginger and fry until the onion is golden brown.

3 Add the ground spices (coriander, roasted cumin, red chilli, turmeric), the tomatoes, yoghurt, coconut and salt to the pan. Stir the mixture over the heat for 2 minutes.

4 Add the prawns and cook on medium heat until all the liquid has been absorbed and the oil appears on the surface of the mixture.

5 Do not stir too frequently or the prawns will become mushy. Remove the pan from the heat. Sprinkle over the garam masala, green chilli and chopped coriander leaves. Set the pan on one side while the rice is cooking.

6 Arrange the cooked rice and prawns in layers in a larger pan. Pour in the milk and heat gently for 3 minutes to absorb the liquid. Tip the contents from the cooking dish into the serving dish before serving.

SERVING SUGGESTION:

Serve hot with yoghurt, kerala (bitter gourd), aubergine, moong ki hari dal and chapati.

DUM ALOO

WHOLE FRIED POTATO IN SAUCE

SERVES: 4

Dum Aloo curry is popular in all parts of India. In southern and eastern India coconut is added and in western parts sugar and lemon are added to the dish. It is one of the cheapest but tastiest curries.

INGREDIENTS:	METRIC	IMPERIAL	AMERICAN
Large onion	1	1	1
Large garlic cloves	3	3	3
Fresh ginger	1.2 cm	$1/2$ in	$1/2$ in

Wash the onion, garlic and ginger and cut them in large pieces. Combine all in a blender to make a fine paste.

Small potatoes	500 g	1 lb 2 oz	4 $1/2$ cups
Ghee or oil	60 ml	4 tbsp	$1/4$ cup
Small onion, finely chopped	1	1	1
Bay leaves	2	2	2
*Black cardamom	1	1	1
*Cinnamon stick	1.2 cm	$1/2$ in	$1/2$ in
*Cloves	4	4	4
*Peppercorns	4	4	4
Ground coriander/cilantro	10 ml	2 tsp	2 tsp
Ground roasted cumin	2.5 ml	$1/2$ tsp	$1/2$ tsp
Ground red chilli	2.5 ml	$1/2$ tsp	$1/2$ tsp
Ground turmeric	2.5 ml	$1/2$ tsp	$1/2$ tsp
Garam masala	2.5 ml	$1/2$ tsp	$1/2$ tsp
Tomatoes, tinned	400 g	14 oz	$1 3/4$ cups
Salt to taste			
Natural yoghurt	150 ml	$1/4$ pt	$2/3$ cup

TO GARNISH:

Garam masala	2.5 ml	½ tsp	½ tsp
Green coriander/cilantro leaves, chopped	15 ml	1 tbsp	1 tbsp
Green chilli, chopped	1	1	1

COOKING TIME: 50 MINUTES

1 Peel the potatoes. Prick them all over with a fork then fry over a medium heat until golden brown. Set them to one side.

2 Heat the ghee or oil in a heavy-bottomed saucepan on medium heat. Add the chopped onion and the whole spices and fry gently until golden brown.

3 Stir in the blended mixture and fry again until golden brown.

4 Then add the ground spices, tomatoes and salt and cook until the ghee/oil appears on top of the mixture.

5 Stir in the yoghurt and cook until all the liquid has been absorbed.

6 Add 250 ml/8 fl oz/1 cup water and the fried potatoes. Bring it to the boil, reduce the heat to low, cover the pan and cook for 10 minutes or until tender.

7 Sprinkle over the garnish before serving.

SERVING SUGGESTIONS:

Serve hot with dahi bara, khatéwalé kabuli channa, bhutoora or puri.

STEP 4

DAHI BARA

MAKES: 11

This is a cool yoghurt dish for a party or special occasion. It is eaten at any meal and as one of the items of chāt with tamarind chutney. Although it is loved and cooked in every corner of India, it is a speciality and pride of northern India.

INGREDIENTS:	METRIC	IMPERIAL	AMERICAN
Urud ki dhuli dal	75 g	3 oz	1/2 cup
Moong ki dhuli dal and channa dal	25 g	1 oz	1 tbsp
Water	125 ml	5 fl oz	1/2 cup
Garam masala	2.5 ml	1/2 tsp	1/2 tsp
Ground ginger	1.25 ml	1/4 tsp	1/4 tsp
Ground red chilli	1.25 ml	1/4 tsp	1/4 tsp
Asafoetida	1.25 ml	1/4 tsp	1/4 tsp
Oil for frying			

1 Clean the dals then soak together for 3–4 hours.

2 Wash and drain the dals, then combine with the water in a blender and blend to make a thick smooth paste. Whip until spongy. (Take a cupful of cold water and drop about 2.5 ml/½tsp dal mixture into it. If it floats on top it means the mixture is nice and spongy.)

3 Add all the ground spices and asafoetida and mix well.

FRYING TIME: 30 MINUTES

1 Heat the oil in a deep frying pan (skillet) on a medium heat.

2 Place some cold water on your left palm and put about 15ml/1 tbsp of the lentil mixture on it. Flatten it to about 3 mm/⅛ in thick and make a hole in the centre with your finger (so that it can cook from the inside).

3 Gently turn it over on your right hand fingers and slip it in the hot oil.

4 Fry 5 or 6 baras together until golden brown on both sides. Take them out with a slotted spoon and place them on a cooling tray.

5 If you find it difficult to shape by the above method then drop 15 ml/1 tbsp of the lentil mixture in such a way that it forms a patty about 5 cm/2 in diameter and 3 mm/⅛ in thick.

6 Boil 1.2 litres/2 pts/5 cups water in a saucepan and add the fried bara. Leave to soak for 20 minutes.

7 Take out a bara, place it on your palm and press with the other, squeezing out excess water without changing the shape of the baras.

TO GARNISH:

Ground roasted cumin	10 ml	2 tsp	2 tsp
Salt to taste			
Natural yoghurt, whipped	600 ml	1 pt	2½ cups
Green coriander/cilantro leaves, chopped	30 ml	2 tbsp	2 tbsp
Small green chilli, chopped	1	1	1

1 Mix 5 ml/1 tsp roasted cumin and the salt into the whipped yoghurt.

2 Take a bara, dip it in the yoghurt and place it in a serving dish.

3 Arrange all the baras likewise on a dish and pour over the remaining yoghurt. Keep it in the refrigerator for 1–2 hours before serving. Sprinkle over the rest of the cumin then the remaining garnish before serving.

SERVING SUGGESTION:

Serve cold with tamarind chutney, pulao, puri or bhutoora, any vegetable or meat dish, and chickpeas/ garbanzos.

STEP 4

BHUTOORA

MAKES: 20

Bhutoora is one of the special and original breads of Punjab. The appetite increases when one sees the bhutoora swelling like a balloon while they are being fried!

INGREDIENTS:	METRIC	IMPERIAL	AMERICAN
Yeast, dried	5 ml	1 tsp	1 tsp
Sugar	5 ml	1 tsp	1 tsp
Water, lukewarm	30 ml	2 tbsp	2 tbsp

Place the above ingredients in a small bowl. Mix with a fork, cover and leave in a warm place for 30 minutes. It should rise and foam up.

Margarine	25 g	1 oz	2 tbsp
Plain/all-purpose flour, sifted	500 g	1 lb	$4\frac{1}{2}$ cups
Natural yoghurt	100 ml	$3\frac{1}{2}$ fl oz	$6\frac{1}{2}$ tbsp
Large pinch of salt			
Water, lukewarm	100 ml	$3\frac{1}{2}$ fl oz	$6\frac{1}{2}$ fl oz
Oil for frying			

1 Rub the margarine into the flour.

2 Add the yoghurt, salt and the risen yeast and mix thoroughly.

3 Knead the dough with warm water for about 5 minutes or until the dough is springy and satiny.

4 Cover and leave in a warm place for 3–4 hours or until the dough has risen to double its original size.

COOKING TIME: 30 MINUTES

1 Divide the dough into about 20 equal portions.

2 Take a portion of dough and roll into a ball.

3 Put a little oil on the palm of your hands and flatten the ball, turning quickly from one palm to the other, until it is 5 mm/¼ in thin (some people like it even thinner) or roll it out like puri with a rolling pin.

4 Heat the oil in a deep frying pan (skillet) on high heat.

5 Slip the bhutoora into the hot oil from the edge of the pan.

6 Gently press the bhutoora with a slotted spoon all over and it will rise like a balloon.

7 Fry both sides light brown. I roll another bhutoora while one is frying.

SERVING SUGGESTION:

Serve with khatéwalé kabuli chunna, dahi bara, matar paneer, cauliflower or stuffed aubergine/eggplant. The bhutoora can be reheated under the grill.

This is only the fifth step but I am going to throw you in at the deep end. Hard work, yes, but by the end of this step you'll be able to hold a grand party or a banquet with great pride. I am sure that you'll charm your friends with your culinary expertise.

Stuffed Murgh Musallum is a wedding-party dish. Pumpkin Ka Kofta is a vegetarian dish suitable for any special occasion. You will also learn how to make Roghni Naan in my own personal style and Stuffed Naan. There is also a delicious recipe for cooking bitter gourd. Lassi is a yoghurt drink. It is a speciality of Punjab but is very popular all over India.

STEP 5

STUFFED MURGH MUSALLUM

CHICKEN WITH NUTS, MINCED LAMB AND RICE

SERVES: 4–6

*S*tuffed Murgh Musallum is one of the royal chicken dishes which is very nourishing, attractive and tasty. The sauce is optional. The dish is hot.

INGREDIENTS:	METRIC	IMPERIAL	AMERICAN
Medium chicken	1	1	1

PREPARING THE MARINADE:

Large garlic cloves	6	6	6
Fresh ginger	4 cm	$1^1/_2$ in	$1^1/_2$ in
Dried figs	2	2	2
Small green chilli (optional)	1	1	1
Lemon juice	30 ml	2 tbsp	2 tbsp
Sugar	10 ml	2 tsp	2 tsp
Garam masala	10 ml	2 tsp	2 tsp
Ground coriander/cilantro	10 ml	2 tsp	2 tsp
Ground red chilli	2.5 ml	$^1/_2$ tsp	$^1/_2$ tsp
Ground turmeric	2.5 ml	$^1/_2$ tsp	$^1/_2$ tsp
Ground black pepper	1.25 ml	$^1/_4$ tsp	$^1/_4$ tsp
Ground cumin	5 ml	1 tsp	1 tsp
Salt to taste			
Natural yoghurt	150 ml	$^1/_4$ pt	$1^1/_4$ cups

1 Skin, wash and prick the chicken all over with a fork.

2 Combine the marinade ingredients in a blender and blend to make a smooth paste. Rub the paste all over the chicken and marinate for 3 hours.

PREPARING THE FILLING:

Ghee	*60 ml*	*4 tbsp*	*4 tbsp*
Medium onion, thinly sliced	*1*	*1*	*1*
Lamb or mutton, minced	*200 g*	*7 oz*	*1¾ cup*
Rice (basmati or patna), cleaned washed and drained	*200 g*	*7 oz*	*1 cup*
Raisins	*100 g*	*4 oz*	*¼ cup*
Almonds, blanched and cut in half lengthwise	*50 g*	*2 oz*	*¼ cup*
Cashew-nuts, cut in half lengthwise	*50 g*	*2 oz*	*¼ cup*
Pistachios	*25 g*	*1 oz*	*¼ cup*
Peas, frozen	*200 g*	*7 oz*	*1 cup*
Fresh dill	*15 ml*	*1 tbsp*	*1 tbsp*
OR dried dill	*7.5 ml*	*½ tbsp*	*½ tbsp*
Saffron	*2.5 ml*	*½ tsp*	*½ tsp*
Ground coriander/cilantro	*10 ml*	*2 tsp*	*2 tsp*
Garam masala	*10 ml*	*2 tsp*	*2 tsp*
Aniseed	*5 ml*	*1 tsp*	*1 tsp*
Ground red chilli	*2.5 ml*	*½ tsp*	*½ tsp*
Ground turmeric	*2.5 ml*	*½ tsp*	*½ tsp*
Salt to taste			
Water	*500 ml*	*18 fl oz*	*2 cups*

COOKING TIME: 45 MINUTES

1 For best roasting effect place the marinated chicken on skewers or on a wire rack, sprinkle over 10 ml/2 tsp oil and place in a preheated oven on 200°C/400°F/gas mark 6 and roast for 45 minutes or until cooked. Turn the chicken over 2 or 3 times and baste with the marinade. Prepare the stuffing while the chicken is roasting.

2 Heat the ghee in a large heavy-bottomed saucepan on medium heat and fry the onion gently until golden brown.

3 Add the minced lamb and fry for 3 minutes.

4 Put in the rice and fry for a further 2 minutes.

5 Mix in the raisins, almonds, cashew-nuts, pistachios, peas, dill, saffron, coriander, garam masala, aniseed, red chilli, turmeric, salt and water.

6 Bring to the boil, reduce the heat to minimum, close the lid and cook for 10 minutes or until the meat and the rice are tender and all the water has been absorbed. Turn the heat off.

7 Stuff the chicken tightly with the filling mixture.

8 Prepare the sauce while the filling is cooking. (It can be prepared the day before.)

MAKING THE SAUCE:

Large garlic cloves	5	5	5
Medium onions, finely chopped	4	4	4
Fresh ginger, chopped	2.5 cm	1 in	1 in
Water	45 ml	3 tbsp	3 tbsp
Oil	150 ml	10 tbsp	$\frac{2}{3}$ cup
Cumin seeds	5 ml	1 tsp	1 tsp
Bay leaves	2	2	2
*Cloves	6	6	6
*Peppercorns	6	6	6
*Black cardamom	2	2	2
*Cinnamon stick	2.5 cm	1 in	1 in
Ground almonds	15 ml	1 tbsp	1 tbsp
Ground coriander/cilantro	15 ml	1 tbsp	1 tbsp
Ground roasted cumin	10 ml	2 tsp	2 tsp
Ground red chilli	2.5 ml	$\frac{1}{2}$ tsp	$\frac{1}{2}$ tsp
Tomatoes, tinned	400 g	14 oz	$1\frac{3}{4}$ cups
Salt to taste			
Lemon juice	30 ml	2 tbsp	2 tbsp

1 Combine three-quarters of the onion, the garlic, ginger and water in a blender and blend to make a smooth paste (you do not require water if you are using a food processor).

TO GARNISH:

Eggs, hard-boiled/hard-cooked	6	6	6
Green coriander/cilantro leaves, chopped	30 ml	2 tbsp	2 tbsp
Small green chilli, chopped	1	1	1

COOKING TIME: 30 MINUTES

1 Heat the oil in a large heavy-bottomed saucepan on medium heat and brown the cumin seeds. Add the remaining chopped onion, bay leaves, cloves, peppercorns, black cardamoms and cinnamon stick, and fry gently until golden brown.

2 Put in the blended paste and fry for a further few minutes until golden brown.

3 Stir in the almonds, coriander, roasted cumin, red chilli, tomatoes and salt and cook until all the liquid has been absorbed.

4 Mix in the lemon juice and cook again until all the liquid is evaporated and the oil appears on the surface of the mixture.

5 Pour in 200 ml/7 fl oz/scant 1 cup water. Bring to the boil. Place the stuffed chicken in the sauce and baste the chicken with the sauce for a further 10 minutes on a medium-low heat (gently turn over twice) or until all the water has been absorbed.

SERVING SUGGESTION:

Place the cooked chicken on a large flat serving dish. Arrange the left-over filling around it. Halve the eggs and place on top. Sprinkle over the garnish before serving.

V

PUMPKIN KA KOFTA

PUNJABI-STYLE PUMPKIN

SERVES: 6 (MAKES: 12)

Pumpkin Ka Kofta is one of the best pumpkin dishes. It used to be prepared in our house in India for a Sunday meal, a party or a special occasion. My father would eat pumpkin only in the Kofta form. You will find the dish to be medium-hot.

INGREDIENTS:	METRIC	IMPERIAL	AMERICAN
Pumpkin, peeled, washed and grated	1 kg	2 lb 4 oz	2 lb 4 oz
Gram flour, sifted and lightly roasted on a flat pan	100 g	4 oz	1 cup
Green coriander/cilantro leaves, chopped	30 ml	2 tbsp	2 tbsp
Garam masala	5 ml	1 tsp	1 tsp
Ground red chilli	2.5 ml	½ tsp	½ tsp
Green chilli, finely chopped	1	1	1
Salt to taste			
Dried prunes, seeds removed	12	12	12
Oil for frying			

1 Place the grated pumpkin in a saucepan with 250 ml/8 fl oz/1 cup water on a high heat bring it to the boil, reduce to medium heat and cook for 40 minutes or until tender. Dry off any remaining water on a high heat. Leave to cool.

2 Place all the remaining ingredients except the prunes and the oil in a bowl with the pumpkin. Mix it thoroughly, if needed add a little water to combine (like a dough).

3 Heat the oil in a deep frying pan (skillet) on a medium heat.

STEP 5

4 While the oil is heating, divide the pumpkin mixture into 12 equal portions.

5 Roll them into balls, flatten, place a prune in the centre of each, bring the edges over to cover and form into an oblong.

6 Deep-fry 6 koftas together until golden brown. Keep them aside until the sauce is ready.

PREPARING THE SAUCE:

Large garlic cloves	3	3	3
Fresh ginger	2.5 cm	1 in	1 in
Medium onion, coarsely chopped	1	1	1

Combine the garlic, ginger and onion in a blender with 45 ml/3 tbsp water and blend to make a smooth paste.

Oil or ghee	90 ml	6 tbsp	$\frac{1}{2}$ cup
*Cloves	4	4	4
*Peppercorns	4	4	4
Bay leaves	2	2	2
*Black cardamom	1	1	1
*Cinnamon stick	1.2 cm	$\frac{1}{2}$ in	$\frac{1}{2}$ in
Poppy seeds, ground	10 ml	2 tsp	2 tsp
Ground coriander/cilantro	5 ml	1 tsp	1 tsp
Ground roasted cumin	5 ml	1 tsp	1 tsp
Garam masala	5 ml	1 tsp	1 tsp
Ground turmeric	2.5 ml	$\frac{1}{2}$ tsp	$\frac{1}{2}$ tsp
Ground red chilli	1.5 ml	$\frac{1}{4}$ tsp	$\frac{1}{4}$ tsp
Ground mace	1.5 ml	$\frac{1}{4}$ tsp	$\frac{1}{4}$ tsp
Ground nutmeg	1.5 ml	$\frac{1}{4}$ tsp	$\frac{1}{4}$ tsp
Tomatoes, tinned	400 g	14 oz	$1\frac{3}{4}$ cups
Salt to taste			
Water	200 ml	7 fl oz	1 cup

TO GARNISH:

Garam masala	2.5 ml	½ tsp	½ tsp
Green coriander/cilantro leaves, chopped	15 ml	1 tbsp	1 tbsp
Small green chilli, chopped	1	1	1

COOKING TIME: 30 MINUTES

1 Heat the ghee or oil in a large heavy-bottomed saucepan and gently fry the whole spices until they are golden brown.

2 Add the ground paste and fry for a further few minutes until golden brown.

3 Mix in the poppy seeds and fry for 2 minutes.

4 Stir in the ground spices and then the tomatoes and salt and cook until all the liquid has been absorbed and the oil/ghee appears on the surface of the mixture.

5 Pour in the water, bring to the boil, add the fried kofta and reduce the heat to low and simmer for 2 minutes only.

6 Sprinkle over the garnish before serving.

SERVING SUGGESTION:

Serve hot with pulao, rayta, puri, stuffed aubergine/ eggplant and dal.

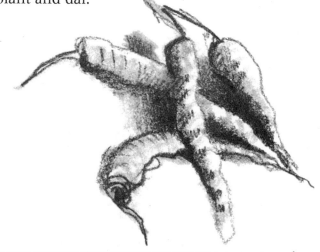

STEP 5

❊ BITTER GOURD WITH ONION

SERVES: 4

This is one of the easiest, simplest and the quickest ways of cooking bitter gourd. It is delicious, a little crunchy and one can keep it in a refrigerator for a week. You'll find this dish to be medium-hot.

INGREDIENTS:	METRIC	IMPERIAL	AMERICAN
Bitter gourd, cut into rounds 5 mm/¼ in thick	250 g	9 oz	2¼ cups

Place in a saucepan with 200ml/7 fl oz/scant/cup water, bring to the boil, then drain. Repeat twice. This will help to remove the bitterness.

Oil	75 ml	5 tbsp	5 tbsp
Small onion, thinly sliced	4	4	4
Small green chilli, chopped	1	1	1
Ground coriander/cilantro	5 ml	1 tsp	1 tsp
Ground roasted cumin	5 ml	1 tsp	1 tsp
Garam masala	5 ml	1 tsp	1 tsp
Ground red chilli	2.5 ml	½ tsp	½ tsp
Ground turmeric	2.5 ml	½ tsp	½ tsp
Salt to taste			

COOKING TIME: 30 MINUTES

1 Heat the oil in a frying pan (skillet) on a medium-low heat. Add the onion, chilli and the bitter gourd and fry for 25 minutes or until golden brown and crispy (do not cook too quickly).

2 Stir in all the ground spices and salt and cook for 5 minutes on a low heat. Turn the heat off.

SERVING SUGGESTION

Serve hot or cold with paratha or puri, urud dal, rice and rayta.

ROGHNI NAAN

MAKES: 12

In India people cook the naan bread in a tandoor. If one isn't available it can be baked in an oven.

INGREDIENTS:	METRIC	IMPERIAL	AMERICAN
Yeast, dried	10 ml	2 tsp	2 tsp
Sugar	10 ml	2 tsp	2 tsp
Water, lukewarm	30 ml	2 tbsp	2 tbsp

Place the above ingredients in a small bowl. Mix with a fork, cover and leave in a warm place for 30 minutes. It should rise and foam up.

	METRIC	IMPERIAL	AMERICAN
Margarine or ghee	25 g	1 oz	2 tbsp
Bicarbonate of soda/baking soda	1.5 ml	$\frac{1}{4}$ tsp	$\frac{1}{4}$ tsp
Plain/all-purpose flour, sifted	500 g	1 lb 2 oz	$4\frac{1}{2}$ cups
Large pinch of salt			
Natural yoghurt	30 ml	2 tbsp	2 tbsp
Milk, warm	125 ml	4 fl oz	$\frac{1}{2}$ cup

1 Rub the margarine and the bicarbonate of soda into the flour.

2 Add the salt, yoghurt and the risen yeast and mix thoroughly.

3 Knead the dough with warm milk for 5 minutes or until the dough is springy and satiny.

4 Cover and leave in a warm place for 3–4 hours or until the dough has risen to double the original size.

TO FINISH:

	METRIC	IMPERIAL	AMERICAN
Milk to brush	15 ml	1 tbsp	1 tbsp
Sesame seeds	15 ml	1 tbsp	1 tbsp
Onion seeds (kalonji)	15 ml	1 tbsp	1 tbsp

COOKING TIME: 9 MINUTES

1 Heat an oven to 240°C/475°F/gas mark 9.

2 Roll half of the dough into a 15 cm/6 in long strip. Divide it into 6 equal portions. Repeat with the rest of the dough.

3 Take a portion and flatten it with your palm into an oval shape about 5 mm/¼ in thick.

4 Place 4 or 5 naans on to a greased baking tray. Brush the tops with milk and sprinkle over the sesame and the onion seeds. Repeat with the rest of the naan.

5 Bake for 7 minutes, then reverse the position of the trays and bake for a further 2 minutes or until golden brown.

SERVING SUGGESTION:

Serve hot with any tandoori dish and khatéwalé kabuli chunna.

STUFFED NAAN

MAKES: 8

This recipe makes a naan which will not require you to prepare the dough a couple of hours beforehand. Still your naans will be perfect. Make the dough just before you start preparing the rest of your meal.

PREPARING THE DOUGH:

INGREDIENTS:	METRIC	IMPERIAL	AMERICAN
Margarine	25 g	1 oz	2 tbsp
Natural yoghurt	30 ml	2 tbsp	2 tbsp
Bicarbonate of soda/baking soda	2.5 ml	$\frac{1}{2}$ tsp	$\frac{1}{2}$ tsp
Small pinch of salt			
Self-raising/self-rising flour	300 g	11 oz	$2\frac{3}{4}$ cups
Milk	100 ml	$3\frac{1}{2}$ fl oz	$\frac{1}{3}$ cup

1 Rub the margarine, yoghurt, bicarbonate of soda and salt into the flour.

2 Knead the dough with milk for about 2 minutes or until the dough is springy and satiny (you may need a little more than ⅓ cup).

3 Cover and leave for at least 30 minutes.

PREPARING THE FILLING:

Potatoes, boiled in jackets, peeled and then mashed	450 g	1 lb	2 cups
Green coriander/cilantro leaves, chopped	30 ml	2 tbsp	2 tbsp
Lemon juice	30 ml	2 tbsp	2 tbsp
Garam masala	5 ml	1 tsp	1 tsp
Ground red chilli	2.5 ml	$\frac{1}{2}$ tsp	$\frac{1}{2}$ tsp
Small onion, finely chopped	1	1	1
Small green chilli, finely chopped	1	1	1
Salt to taste			

Mix all the ingredients for the filling in a bowl and divide into 8 equal portions.

COOKING TIME: 24 MINUTES

1 Divide the dough into 8 equal portions.

2 Take a piece of dough, flatten it and make a round by patting it with your hand.

3 Place 1 portion of filling on it and cover by bringing the edges together.

4 Again flatten it with your hand and make a teardrop or a round shape. It should be about 5 mm/¼ in thick.

5 Grease the grill tray with oil. My tray takes 3 naans at a time.

6 Place the naans on the tray, brush the tops with water (I usually wet my hand under the tap and wet the top of the naan before placing it on the tray).

7 Grill them until golden brown.

8 Turn them over and smear the top again with water and cook the other side golden brown as well.

9 Take the naan out and smear the top with butter or ghee.

10 One tray of naans should take about 5 minutes.

SERVING SUGGESTION:

Serve hot with any curry.

✳ LASSI

YOGHURT DRINK

MAKES: 6 GLASSES

This refreshing cool drink is enjoyed during the summer at breakfast (instead of tea) and at lunch time (instead of water) in India. It can be sweet or salty.

INGREDIENTS:	METRIC	IMPERIAL	AMERICAN
Natural yoghurt	450 ml	$^{3}/_{4}$ pt	2 cups
Sugar	60 g	4 tbsp	4 tbsp
Water, cold	100 ml	$3^{1}/_{2}$ fl oz	$6^{1}/_{2}$ tbsp
Ice cubes (quantity depends upon weather)	12	12	12

PREPARATION TIME: 5 MINUTES

1 Combine the yoghurt and the sugar in a blender and blend for 2 minutes or until smooth.

2 Add the water and the ice cubes and blend for a further 1 minute or until a lot of foam appears (be careful not to blend for too long otherwise you may get butter and whey from the yoghurt!).

SERVING SUGGESTION:

Drink sweetened lassi at breakfast with paratha/ pudha/pakora/puri-aloo. For other meals, especially during lunch, Indians drink salty lassi because, due to the heat, they lose a lot of salt in perspiration. To make salty lassi, use the same recipe except add salt, 5 ml/1 tsp ground roasted cumin, 1.5 ml/$^{1}/_{4}$ tsp black pepper instead of the sugar and add 120 ml/4 fl oz/$^{1}/_{2}$ cup extra water to the yoghurt.

In this step you can increase your repertoire of sweets, chutneys and snacks/starters.

My mother's style of Stuffed Bread Rolls are admired by everyone – young and old alike. They have a lovely tangy, spicy filling of potato, peas, onions and raisins. My son Sumeet is very fond of Gulab Jamun which are rich in protein and carbohydrate.

STUFFED BREAD ROLLS

MAKES: 18

B read rolls are an extremely tasty, nourishing and filling snack/starter. You will find the recipe to be medium-hot.

INGREDIENTS:	METRIC	IMPERIAL	AMERICAN
Potatoes, boiled in jackets, peeled and mashed	500 g	1 lb 2 oz	2¼ cups
Frozen peas, thawed	250 g	9 oz	2¼ cups
OR fresh peas, cooked in water until tender	250 g	9 oz	2¼ cups
Medium onion, finely chopped	1	1	1
Small green chilli, chopped	1	1	1
Raisins	100 g	4 oz	¾ cup
Lemon juice	30 ml	2 tbsp	2 tbsp
Green coriander/cilantro leaves, chopped	30 ml	2 tbsp	2 tbsp
Garam masala	5 ml	1 tsp	1 tsp
Ground red chilli	2.5 ml	½ tsp	½ tsp
Salt to taste			

1 Place the mashed potatoes, peas, onion, green chilli, raisins, lemon, coriander leaves and the garam masala, red chilli and salt into a large bowl and mix them well.

2 Divide them into 18 equal portions. Roll them round and give them an oblong shape. Set them to one side.

Bread, white thin slices cut in halves	9	9	9
Oil for frying			

COOKING TIME: 30 MINUTES

1 Fill a saucepan with warm water. Put a half slice of bread in it and soak for about 10–15 seconds.

2 Take out the soaked bread (put another piece of bread in the water) and place on to the left palm of your hand. Press it gently with your right hand palm and squeeze out all the water.

3 Place 1 portion of potato mixture on to the squeezed bread. Gently roll the bread around the mixture. Keep pressing the edges so that the filling won't come out. Make more while the oil is heating.

4 Heat the oil in a deep frying pan (skillet) on medium heat. Fry 3 or 4 stuffed bread rolls together until they are golden brown. I stuff the bread pieces for the next batch while the first is frying.

SERVING SUGGESTION:

Serve hot at tea with chutney, gulab jamun and barfi, or as a starter.

GULAB JAMUN

MAKES: 12

The Gulab Jamun is a delicious and popular sweet of India. It is served at almost all parties and special occasions. You can also make it without filling.

INGREDIENTS:	METRIC	IMPERIAL	AMERICAN
Full cream milk powder	100 g	4 oz	1¼ cups
Ghee, melted	30 ml	2 tbsp	2 tbsp
Plain/all-purpose white flour	15 ml	1 tbsp	1 tbsp
Semolina/cream of wheat	15 ml	1 tbsp	1 tbsp
Milk, lukewarm	105 ml	7 tbsp	7 tbsp

Place the milk powder, ghee, flour and semolina in a bowl and mix thoroughly. Pour in the milk and make a soft dough. Cover and leave for 20 minutes.

FOR THE FILLING:

Ghee and oil to fry (equal quantities)			
Sultanas/golden raisins	15 g	½ oz	1 tbsp
Almonds, blanched and finely chopped	6	6	6
Pistachios, finely chopped	5	5	5
Ground green cardamoms	2.5 ml	½ tsp	½ tsp

Combine all the above ingredients to make the filling.

FOR THE SYRUP:

Sugar	250 g	9 oz	2 ¼ cups
Water	250 ml	8 fl oz	1 cup

COOKING TIME: 30 MINUTES

1 Heat the ghee and oil together in a deep frying pan (skillet) on medium-low heat.

2 While the fat is heating, divide the dough into 12 equal parts and roll into small balls.

3 Flatten each one, place on a little filling and roll them round again.

4 Add 6 balls to the frying pan (skillet) and gently fry until golden brown. Keep on turning them over (don't fry them too quickly otherwise they will not be cooked inside. If the fat is too hot reduce the heat to low). Take them out with a slotted spoon and place them on a cooling tray. Repeat until all of them are fried.

5 While you are frying the gulab jamun, place the sugar and water in a saucepan to boil on medium heat. Turn the heat off as soon as the sugar has dissolved.

6 Add the fried gulab jamun to the syrup. Bring them to the boil again on medium heat, then reduce to a low heat and cook for a further 5 minutes.

SERVING SUGGESTION:

Serve hot or cold after the meal and at tea time with samosa, pakora or bread rolls.

V

DHANIYA CHUTNEY

FILLS: 450 G /1 LB JAM JAR

This chutney has an exquisite and individual flavour. It is a hot recipe.

INGREDIENTS:	METRIC	IMPERIAL	AMERICAN
Bunch of coriander/cilantro leaves, washed and leaves and the tender stems coarsely cut	1	1	1
Medium onion, coarsely chopped	1	1	1
Small green chilli	1	1	1
Large lemon, juice extracted	1	1	1
Ground red chilli	2.5 ml	1/2 tsp	1/2 tsp
Salt to taste			

PREPARATION TIME: 10 MINUTES

Combine all the ingredients in a blender and blend to make a fine paste. Add more lemon juice if necessary.

SERVING SUGGESTION:

Serve at meals and at tea with samosa, bread rolls, pakora, kabab and mathi etc. The dhaniya chutney will keep about one week in a clean, airtight jar or container in a fridge.

In this step you will learn to make Pork Vindaloo. The pork can also be substituted by lamb or chicken. Sabat Moong Ki Hari Dal (whole green mung beans) is cooked in a Punjabi style. The texture should neither be too thick nor too runny.

Bharwa Bengun is an aubergine dish that is a firm favourite with my family. Kulfi is one of my favourite ice creams. When I came to Britain I did not have time to prepare Kulfi the traditional way, so I tried different combinations of cream without much success. Fifteen years ago I found this combination of an alternative to real cream and evaporated milk produced exactly the right textured mixture. Falooda is an optional garnish for Kulfi. It can also be served as a drink.

PORK OR LAMB VINDALOO

SERVES: 4–6

*I*n this dish I have specially roasted the ingredients to obtain a dark colour and the finest possible flavour. The dish would be suitable for a party meal and is very hot.

INGREDIENTS:	METRIC	IMPERIAL	AMERICAN
Whole coriander/cilantro, cleaned	15 ml	1 tbsp	1tbsp
Cumin seeds	10 ml	2 tsp	2 tsp
Mustard seeds	10 ml	2 tsp	2tsp
Peppercorns	5	5	5
Cloves	5	5	5
Small dried red chillies, broken into a few pieces	4	4	4
Cinnamon stick	2.5 cm	1 in	1 in
Black cardamom, seeds only	1	1	1

Heat a flat frying pan (skillet) on medium heat and roast all the spices until brown. Grind them in a grinder to a fine powder.

Ground turmeric	2.5 ml	$^1/_2$ tsp	$^1/_2$ tsp
Salt to taste			

Mix the turmeric and salt in the roasted powder.

Large garlic cloves, chopped	5	5	5
Fresh ginger, chopped	4 cm	$1^1/_2$ in	$1^1/_2$ in
Vinegar	60 ml	4 tbsp	4 tbsp
Pork or lamb, cut into 5 cm/2 in pieces, fat trimmed and washed	500 g	1lb 2 oz	$4^1/_2$ cups

Combine all the chopped and roasted ingredients in a blender and blend to make a smooth paste with the vinegar. Rub the paste into the meat pieces and leave to marinate overnight.

Oil	75ml	5 tbsp	5 tbsp
Medium onions, finely chopped	2	2	2
Tomatoes, tinned	400 g	14 oz	1 ¾ cups
Vinegar (optional)	150 ml	5 fl oz	⅔ cup

TO GARNISH:

Garam masala	2.5 ml	½ tsp	½ tsp
Green coriander/cilantro leaves, chopped	15 ml	1 tbsp	1 tbsp
Green chilli, chopped	1	1	1

COOKING TIME: 1 HOUR 10 MINUTES

1 Heat the oil in a large heavy-bottomed saucepan on medium heat and gently fry the onions until golden brown.

2 Add the marinated meat and fry for a further 15 minutes or until golden brown.

3 Stir in the tomatoes and fry until all the liquid has been absorbed and the oil appears on the surface of the mixture.

4 Put in the vinegar, if using, and 250 ml/8 fl oz/1 cup water. Bring to the boil. Close the lid, reduce the heat to medium-low and cook for 40 minutes or until the meat is tender.

5 Sprinkle over the garnish before serving.

SERVING SUGGESTION:

Serve hot with rice, chapati, rayta and a fried cauliflower or okra dish.

SABAT MOONG KI HARI DAL

WHOLE GREEN MUNG BEANS

SERVES: 4–6

*T*his dal is rich in both taste and protein. It is easily
digested. You will find this dish to be medium-hot.

INGREDIENTS:	METRIC	IMPERIAL	AMERICAN
Whole green mung beans, washed and soaked for an hour	150 g	5 oz	¹/₂ cup
Large pinch of ground turmeric			
Salt to taste			
Water	1.5 litres	3 pts	6 cups

TARKA

Oil or ghee	45 ml	3 tbsp	3 tbsp
Mustard seeds	5 ml	1 tsp	1 tsp
Cumin seeds	5 ml	1 tsp	1 tsp
Medium onion, finely chopped	1	1	1
Fresh ginger, finely chopped	1.2 cm	¹/₂ in	¹/₂ in
Garam masala	5 ml	1 tsp	1 tsp
Ground red chilli	2.5 ml	¹/₂ tsp	¹/₂ tsp
Large pinch of ground turmeric			
Tomatoes, tinned	400 g	14 oz	1³/₄ cups

TO GARNISH:

Green coriander/cilantro leaves, chopped	15 ml	1 tbsp	1 tbsp
Garam masala	2.5 ml	¹/₂ tsp	¹/₂ tsp
Small green chilli, chopped	1	1	1

COOKING TIME: 1 HOUR

1 Place the mung beans, turmeric, salt and the water in a large saucepan. Bring to the boil, skim off any scum and simmer for 50 minutes on medium heat, until tender.

2 While the dal is cooking prepare the tarka. Heat the oil or ghee in a heavy-bottomed saucepan. Add the mustard seeds and when they start crackling add the cumin seeds, then the onion and ginger and fry until golden brown.

3 Add the garam masala, red chilli, turmeric and the tomatoes. Fry until all the water has been absorbed and the oil/ghee appears on the top of the mixture.

4 Stir in the cooked dal and simmer for a further 10 minutes.

5 Sprinkle over the garnish before serving.

SERVING SUGGESTION:

Serve hot with rice, chapati, urud ki sukhi dal, cauliflower, yoghurt and a meat dish.

BHARWA BENGUN

STUFFED BABY AUBERGINE

SERVES: 4–6

Bharwa Bengun is one of the best aubergine/eggplant dishes. Every one loves stuffed aubergine in my family except papa (who is very choosy about vegetables). I vividly remember the time when my youngest brother Binu, as a child, was grabbing the stuffed aubergines with his little hands and the stuffing mixture went all over his face and on his clothes. Papa was annoyed and said, 'You haven't got any brain because you eat too many benguns and the benguns are "begun" (Hindi word meaning worthless).' Binu replied innocently, 'Hurry up and give me one penny and I'll buy the brain from the Punjabi's shop' (a corner sweet shop). Poor papa couldn't hide his smile and the rest of the family burst into laughter.

INGREDIENTS:	METRIC	IMPERIAL	AMERICAN
Large onion, finely chopped	1	1	1
Garlic clove	4	4	4
Fresh ginger	2.5 cm	1 in	1 in

Combine the above and blend them with 45 ml/3 tbsp water into a fine paste.

Oil	80 ml	5 tbsp	5 tbsp
Mustard seeds	2.5 ml	½ tsp	½ tsp
Small onion, finely chopped	1	1	1
Ground coriander/cilantro	5 ml	1 tbsp	1 tbsp
Ground roasted cumin	5 ml	1 tsp	1 tsp
Garam masala	5 ml	1 tsp	1 tsp
Ground red chilli	2.5 ml	½ tsp	½ tsp
Ground turmeric	2.5 ml	½ tsp	½ tsp
Ground nutmeg	1.2 ml	¼ tsp	¼ tsp
Ground mace	1.2 ml	¼ tsp	¼ tsp

Tomatoes, tinned	400 g	14 oz	1¾ cups
Salt to taste			
Tamarind pulp (see page 24)			
OR lemon juice	30 ml	2 tbsp	2 tbsp
Sugar	15 ml	1 tbsp	1 tbsp
Small aubergine/eggplant, washed and slit lengthwise	450 g	1 lb	1 lb
Oil for frying	60 ml	4 tbsp	4 tbsp

TO GARNISH:

Garam masala	2.5 ml	½ tsp	½ tsp
Green coriander/cilantro leaves, chopped	15 ml	1 tbsp	1 tbsp
Small green chilli, chopped	1	1	1

COOKING TIME: 55 MINUTES

1 Heat the oil in a heavy-bottomed saucepan. Add the mustard seeds and fry them until they crackle, then add the chopped onion and fry gently on medium heat until they are golden brown.

2 Stir in the blended paste and fry until golden brown.

3 Add the ground spices, the tomatoes and salt cook until the water has been absorbed and the oil appears on the top of the mixture.

4 Stir in the tamarind pulp and sugar or lemon juice and cook for a further few minutes until all the liquid is absorbed.

5 Cool the mixture and pack it in the aubergines.

6 Heat the oil (for frying) in a frying pan (skillet) on a low heat and put in the stuffed aubergines. Cover the pan and cook, stirring occasionally, for 25 minutes.

7 Place them into a serving dish with the remaining mixture. Sprinkle over the garnish before serving.

SERVING SUGGESTION:

Serve hot with onion paratha, plain rice, whole black lentils, and yoghurt.

KULFI

INDIAN ICE CREAM

SERVES: 4–6

Kulfi is traditionally made by continually reducing milk. However, this is a long and tedious process. I have finally found the perfect combination of creams which can produce the same – if not better – effect. It is also much quicker!

INGREDIENTS:	METRIC	IMPERIAL	AMERICAN
Alternative to real cream (non-dairy cream made with vegetable oil)	300 ml	1/2 pt	1 1/4 cups
Evaporated milk	450 ml	3/4 pt	2 cups
Sugar to taste	60 ml	4 tbsp	4 tbsp
Almonds, blanched and thinly sliced	40 g	1 1/2 oz	1/3 cup
Pistachios, thinly sliced	15 g	1/2 oz	2 tbsp
Essence: rose or kevera water	10 ml	2 tsp	2 tsp
Ground green cardamom	5 ml	1 tsp	1 tsp

1 Whisk the cream, evaporated milk and the sugar until very thick.

2 Add all the ingredients and mix thoroughly.

3 Mix and pour into kulfi containers (conical shaped), or small plastic cups with lids, or empty ice-cream containers can be used instead.

4 Cover and freeze. Stir kulfi every 20–30 minutes to prevent the nuts settling at the bottom.

SERVING SUGGESTION:

Cut kulfi into small rounds and serve cold (with falooda) after a meal.

FALOODA

MAKES: 4 GLASSES

Falooda is used to garnish kulfi (Indian ice cream) and is consumed as a cold drink, especially during the summer. When used as a drink, food colours and lots of crushed ice are added.

INGREDIENTS:	METRIC	IMPERIAL	AMERICAN
Cornflour/cornstarch	50 g	2 oz	1/4 cup
Water	250 ml	9 fl oz	1 cup

FOR THE SYRUP:

Sugar	25 g	1 oz	2 tbsp
Water	50 ml	2 fl oz	1/4 cup
Essence: rose or kevera water	5 ml	1 tsp	1 tsp
Food colour, yellow, red or green	1.5 ml	1/4 tsp	1/4 tsp

Place the water and the sugar on medium heat. Bring to the boil and simmer until the sugar is dissolved. Remove from heat and add the colour and essence when cold.

COOKING TIME: 2 MINUTES

1 Keep iced cold water ready in a bowl. Place a colander on it.

2 Mix the cornflour and the water in a saucepan. Place it on medium heat, stirring constantly. When the mixture is thick and becomes transparent and slightly yellowish remove from heat.

3 Fill a sev/vermicelli machine with the cooked paste. Turn the machine handle swiftly over the sieve in the iced cold water bowl and let the long strands fall on it.

4 Repeat until you have used all the paste.

5 Leave the falooda to set for 1 hour.

6 Lift your colander out and drain out all the water.

7 Add chilled falooda to the syrup.

SERVING SUGGESTION:

Half-fill the glasses with the crushed ice. Then fill them with falooda. Pour over the cold syrup and eat it with a spoon. Also one can garnish one's kulfi by putting falooda over it.

The South Indian bread Dosa with Coconut Chutney is very popular among all all parts of India. It charmed my daughter Sajni even when she was only three years old! She said 'Mummy, this is the yummiest meal I have ever eaten in my whole life!'

Fried fish, Tali Machli, complements Vegetable Pulao. My pulao recipe with cashew-nuts, raisins, peas and long strands of carrot is a delight for both vegetarians and non-vegetarians. It can be garnished with Paneer Tikka. If you are in a rush, it can be eaten with plain yoghurt for a meal.

STEP
8

V

❋ DOSA

SOUTH INDIAN BREAD

D osa is one of the most popular and best breads from southern India. You will find the dish to be medium-hot.

PREPARING THE DOSA MIXTURE:

INGREDIENTS:	METRIC	IMPERIAL	AMERICAN
Rice, cleaned	150 g	5 oz	³/₄ cup
Urdu ki dhuli dal, cleaned	50 g	2 oz	¹/₄ cup

1 Soak the rice and urud dal together in 250 ml lukewarm water for at least 2 hours and blend with the water until smooth.

2 Cover and leave in a warm place to rise for 24 hours.

PREPARING THE FILLING:

Oil	75 ml	5 tbsp	5 tbsp
Mustard seeds	5 ml	1 tsp	1 tsp
Cumin seeds	5 ml	1 tsp	1 tsp
Potatoes, boiled in jackets, peeled and diced	1 kg	2 lb 4 oz	4¹/₄ cups
Garam masala	10 ml	2 tsp	2 tsp
Ground coriander/cilantro	5 ml	1 tsp	1 tsp
Ground roasted cumin	5 ml	1 tsp	1 tsp
Ground ginger	2.5 ml	¹/₂ tsp	¹/₂ tsp
Ground red chilli	2.5 ml	¹/₂ tsp	¹/₂ tsp
Ground turmeric	2.5 ml	¹/₂ tsp	¹/₂ tsp
Salt to taste			
Tomatoes, tinned	400 g	14 oz	1³/₄ cups
Lemon juice	60 ml	4 tbsp	4 tbsp
Coriander/cilantro leaves, chopped	60 ml	4 tbsp	4 tbsp
Small green chilli, chopped	1	1	1
Oil for frying			

DOSA

COOKING TIME: 20 MINUTES

1 Heat the oil in a large heavy-bottomed saucepan on medium heat. Add the mustard seeds and, when they start crackling, brown the cumin seeds.

2 Put in the potato pieces and fry until light brown.

3 Stir in the ground spices (garam masala, coriander, roasted cumin, ginger, red chilli, turmeric), salt and then the tomatoes and cook until all the liquid has been absorbed.

4 Pour in 250 ml/8 fl oz/1 cup water. Bring to the boil. Reduce the heat and simmer for 3 minutes. Add the lemon juice, coriander, and green chilli.

PREPARING THE DOSA:

FRYING TIME: 40 MINUTES

1 Place a flat frying pan (skillet) on medium-low heat. While the pan is heating whip the dosa mixture for 2 minutes, and add a large pinch of salt and 50 ml/ $3^{1}/_{3}$ tbsp water to make a smooth batter.

2 Smear the frying pan with 5 ml/1 tsp oil. Pour on about 45 ml/3 tbsp batter, lift the pan and turn around to spread the batter into a thin circle.

3 Cook for 2 minutes (the edges will begin to leave the pan). Then spoon 10 ml/2 tsp oil around the edges. Turn the dosa over with a flat spoon and pour 10 ml/2 tsp oil as before. Cook both sides light golden brown.

4 Place the dosa on a plate, put 30 ml/2 tbsp hot filling on half the circle and fold over the other half (giving a half moon shape).

5 Continue making dosas till the mixture finishes – one does not need to smear the pan initially for the second dosa.

SERVING SUGGESTION:

Serve hot with coconut chutney and sambar.

COCONUT CHUTNEY

SOUTH INDIAN STYLE

MAKES: 450 G/1 LB JAR

*T*his cooling, refreshing mixture of yoghurt, coconut, mint, coriander leaves and lentil produces a unique taste. The recipe is hot.

INGREDIENTS:	METRIC	IMPERIAL	AMERICAN
Natural yoghurt	150 ml	1/4 pt	2/3 cup
Coconut, desiccated or fresh, grated	75 g	3 oz	1/3 cup
Lemon juice	60 ml	4 tbsp	2 tbsp
Green coriander/cilantro leaves	30 ml	2 tbsp	2 tbsp
Mint leaves	15 ml	1 tbsp	1 tbsp
Gram dal, soaked in warm water for 4 hours	15 ml	1 tbsp	1 tbsp
Ground roasted cumin	5 ml	1 tsp	1 tsp
Ground red chilli	2.5 ml	1/2 tsp	1/2 tsp
Fresh ginger, coarsely chopped	5 mm	1/4 in	1/4 in
Small green chilli	1	1	1
Salt to taste			

Combine all the above ingredients in a blender and blend to make a smooth paste. Place in a bowl.

PREPARING THE TARKA:

Oil	15 ml	1 tbsp	1 tbsp
Large pinch of asafoetida			
Mustard seeds	2.5 ml	1/2 tsp	1/2 tsp
Urud ki dhuli dal, soaked in warm water for 1 hour	5 ml	1 tsp	1 tsp

COCONUT CHUTNEY

COOKING TIME: 2 MINUTES

1 Heat the oil in a small saucepan on medium heat.
   Add the asafoetida and the mustard seeds. When
   the mustard seeds start crackling, fry the urud dal
   until light brown.

2 Pour this over the chutney paste and mix.

SERVING SUGGESTION:

Serve with dosa, sambar and idli.

✲ TALI MACHLI

MARINATED COD FILLETS

SERVES: 4–6

This dish is very popular in the east and on the south coast of India. The piquant spicy flavour of the paste contrasts well with the delicate flavour of the fish. The dish is medium-hot.

INGREDIENTS:	METRIC	IMPERIAL	AMERICAN
Large garlic cloves	5	5	5
Medium onions, coarsely chopped	2	2	2
Fresh ginger	2.5 cm	1 in	1 in
Small green chilli	1	1	1
Vinegar	60 ml	2 fl oz	1/4 cup
Dried pomegranate seeds OR lemon juice (optional)	5 ml	1 tsp	1 tsp

Combine all the above ingredients in a blender and blend to make a smooth paste.

Garam masala	5 ml	1 tsp	1 tsp
Ground roasted cumin	5 ml	1 tsp	1 tsp
Ground red chilli	2.5 ml	1/2 tsp	1/2 tsp
Salt to taste			
Tymol seeds (ajwain), cleaned	5 ml	1 tsp	1 tsp
Cod fillets, skinned, cut into 5 cm/2 in pieces, washed and patted dry	500 g	1 lb 2 oz	18 oz
Oil for frying			

1 Place the blended paste, ground spices (garam masala, roasted cumin, red chilli), salt and the tymol seeds in a large flat dish and mix them well.

2 Add the fish pieces and rub the paste on them thoroughly.

3 Cover and leave them to marinate for 2 hours.

COOKING TIME: 1 HOUR

1 Remove the fish pieces from the marinade and set them on one side.

2 Place the marinade in a saucepan and reduce the liquid on medium heat (it will take about 30 minutes).

3 Coat the fish pieces evenly with the reduced marinade.

4 Heat a flat frying pan (skillet) on medium-low heat. Pour 60 ml/4 tbsp oil in the pan. Put in 4–5 fish pieces and fry gently till golden brown on all sides, taking care not to break them. Turn them over only 2–3 times. Alternatively, sprinkle the fish with oil and place on a greased tray. Grill until golden brown on all sides, turning at least twice.

SERVING SUGGESTION:

Serve hot with vegetable pulao, dal and a potato-bean dish at a meal or at tea with chutney, rasgula and barfi.

VEGETABLE PULAO WITH NUTS

SERVES: 4–6

*T*his dish is a treasure for vegetarians. The combination of nuts, spices and vegetables give it a very distinctive flavour. I always prepare it for a party. This dish is not hot.

INGREDIENTS:	METRIC	IMPERIAL	AMERICAN
Ghee	90 ml	6 tbsp	6 tbsp
Cumin seeds	5 ml	1 tsp	1 tsp
Medium onion, thinly sliced	1	1	1
*Cloves	5	5	5
*Peppercorns	5	5	5
Bay leaves	2	2	2
*Cinnamon stick	2.5 cm	1 in	1 in
Black cardamom	1	1	1
Rice (patna or basmati), cleaned, washed and drained	250 g	9 oz	1 cup
Garam masala	5 ml	1 tsp	1 tsp
Ground mace	1.5 ml	1/4 tsp	1/4 tsp
Ground nutmeg	1.5 ml	1/4 tsp	1/4 tsp
Salt to taste			
Peas, frozen, or fresh shelled	250 g	9 oz	1 cup
Carrots, peeled, washed and grated lengthwise	150 g	5 oz	5 oz
Raisins	75 g	3 oz	1/2 cup
Cashew-nuts, cut in halves lengthwise	50 g	2 oz	1/4 cup
Water	500 ml	18 fl oz	2 cups

COOKING TIME: 45 MINUTES

1 Heat the ghee in a large heavy-bottomed saucepan and brown the cumin seeds. Add the sliced onion, and the whole spices (cloves, peppercorns, bay leaves, cinnamon, black cardamon) and fry until golden brown.

2 Mix in the drained rice and fry for 2 minutes.

3 Stir in the ground spices (garam masala, mace, nutmeg), and the salt and then the peas, carrots, raisins and nuts.

4 Pour in the water. Bring to the boil. Reduce heat to low. Close the lid and cook for 15 minutes. If there is any water left, dry off and cook on high heat (do not stir, but tip the pan a little to check the water). Turn the heat off and leave for at least 5 minutes before serving.

SERVING SUGGESTION:

Serve hot with rayta, a vegetable kofta dish and whole cauliflower.

OPTIONAL GARNISH:

Oil for frying			
Potato, peeled, washed and cut like chips/french fries	*250 g*	*9 oz*	*9 oz*

Heat the oil in a deep frying pan (skillet), and fry the potato chips until crispy golden brown. Garnish the rice with hot chips.

STEP 8

PANEER TIKKA
SPICY CHEESE CHUNKS

MAKES: 10

Paneer Tikka is a wonderful starter for a meal or it can be served as a snack. I also use it to garnish pulao. Paneer is an Indian word for Indian cheese.

INGREDIENTS:	METRIC	IMPERIAL	AMERICAN
Paneer made from 3 pts/1.75 litres/ 7½ cups milk (see page 23)	225 g	8 oz	1 cup
Natural yoghurt	150 ml	¼ pt	⅔ cup
Mint leaves, finely chopped	15 ml	1 tbsp	1 tbsp
Coriander/cilantro leaves, finely chopped	15 ml	1 tbsp	1 tbsp
Sugar	10 ml	2 tsp	2 tsp
Ground roasted cumin	5 ml	1 tsp	1 tsp
Ground coriander/cilantro	5 ml	1 tsp	1 tsp
Garam masala	5 ml	1 tsp	1 tsp
Tymol seeds (ajwain), cleaned	5 ml	1 tsp	1 tsp
Ground red chilli	2.5 ml	½ tsp	½ tsp
Large garlic clove, crushed	1	1	1
Fresh ginger, crushed or grated	1.2 cm	½ in	½ in
Oil	15 ml	1 tbsp	1 tbsp
Salt to taste			

Chop the paneer into 1.2 cm/½ in cubes. Place all the above ingredients, except the oil, in a bowl and rub the mixture thoroughly into the paneer pieces. Leave it to marinate for at least half an hour.

COOKING TIME: 10 MINUTES

1 Empty the bowl contents into a flat frying pan (skillet) and dry off all the liquid.

2 Pour the oil around the paneer chunks.

3 Keep turning every so often and fry until lightly brown.

SERVING SUGGESTION:

Serve hot with dhaniya chutney as a snack, and eat with a cocktail stick/toothpick.

112

This step is devoted to another popular starter known in India as Pakora, but more commonly in the UK as Onion Bhaji. I have written the recipe for this book using a mixture of vegetables. They are very delicious.

Dalmod is often known in the West as Bombay mix. It is an excellent nibble with any kind of drink. Don't get disheartened if you don't have a sev machine. Some members of my evening class improvised a sev machine with an icing bag and colander. It's not brilliant but good enough to start off with – later you can buy one from an Asian grocery shop.

PAKORA

ONION VEGETABLES

SERVES: 4–6

*S*ome Asian restaurants in the UK often sell Pakora by the name of Onion Bhaji which is a misuse of the name. It is one of the delicious snacks which is eaten in every part of India at tea time. One can make the pakoras with one vegetable or a mixture of vegetables.

BATTER:

INGREDIENTS:	METRIC	IMPERIAL	AMERICAN
Gram flour, sifted	250 g	9 oz	$2^{1}/_{4}$ cups
Oil	15 ml	1 tbsp	1 tbsp
Green coriander/cilantro leaves, chopped	30 ml	2 tbsp	2 tbsp
Garam masala	5 ml	1 tsp	1 tsp
Ground red chilli	5 ml	1 tsp	1 tsp
Ground roasted cumin	5 ml	1 tsp	1 tsp
Tymol seeds (ajwain), cleaned	5 ml	1 tsp	1 tsp
Small green chilli, chopped	1	1	1
Salt to taste			
Water, lukewarm	250 ml	8 fl oz	1 cup

1 Place the sifted flour in a bowl and rub the oil into the flour.

2 Add all the above ingredients into the bowl.

3 Gradually pour in 200 ml/7 fl oz/scant 1 cup water to make a thick batter and set the bowl on one side while you cut up the vegetables and onion.

ONION AND VEGETABLE MIXTURE:

Medium onion, thinly sliced	1	1	1
Fenugreek leaves	30 ml	2 tbsp	2 tbsp
OR dried fenugreek	15 ml	1 tbsp	1 tbsp
Spinach, washed and chopped	30 ml	2 tbsp	2 tbsp

Medium potato, peeled and grated	1	1	1
Medium carrot, peeled and grated	1	1	1

Mix the above ingredients together and add to the batter. Add the remaining water if necessary.

COOKING TIME: 25 MINUTES

1 Place the oil in a deep frying pan (skillet) and heat it on medium heat.

2 Put 15 ml/1 tbsp mixture into the hot oil and fry 7 or 8 pakoras together. (If using vegetable pieces dip one by one into the batter and fry 7–8 pieces together.)

3 When they are lightly brown on all sides keep pressing and turning them over until they are cooked and golden brown.

SERVING SUGGESTION:

Serve hot at tea time with tamarind or dhaniya chutney, gulab jamun and barfi. If any pakoras are left over, I reheat them under the grill next day, wrap them in a slice of bread or chapati and enjoy eating them with a cup of tea.

BALUSHAHI

MAKES: 12

Balushahi is a sweet snack. The members of my cookery classes called them doughnuts. One can keep them for a fortnight in an airtight container.

INGREDIENTS:	METRIC	IMPERIAL	AMERICAN
Plain/all-purpose flour, sifted	*200 g*	*7 oz*	*1¾ cups*
Large pinch of bicarbonate of soda/baking soda			
Margarine or ghee	*50 g*	*2 oz*	*2 oz*
Water, lukewarm	*100 ml*	*3½ fl oz*	*6½ tbsp*

Place the flour and the bicarbonate of soda in a bowl. Add the margarine and rub into the flour. Pour in the water and knead until the dough is soft, springy and satiny.

Ghee and oil for frying (mix equal quantities)			
Sugar	*150 g*	*5 oz*	*⅔ cup*
Ground green cardamom	*2.5 ml*	*½ tsp*	*½ tsp*
Water	*100 ml*	*3½ fl oz*	*6½ tbsp*

COOKING TIME: 1 HOUR

1 Heat the ghee and the oil in a deep frying pan (skillet) on a medium heat. While the fat is heating, divide the dough into 12 equal portions. Roll them into balls with the palms of your hands. Flatten them to about 1.2 cm/½ in thick and press in the centre with your finger.

2 Slip the balushahis into the hot fat. Turn the heat off and leave them until the fat stops simmering.

3 Turn them over and heat them again on a medium heat. As soon as the fat starts boiling, turn the heat off. Repeat until the balushahis are risen and they are golden brown. Take them out with slotted spoon and set them on one side.

STEP
9

4 Place the sugar, cardamom and the water in a saucepan. Bring to the boil on a medium heat. As soon as the sugar is dissolved, add the fried balushahis and let them simmer until the syrup is ready to set. (Test by letting a drop of syrup fall into a cup of cold water: if the drop sets at the bottom, it is ready.)

5 Turn the heat off. Keep on turning and coating the balushahis until they are well coated with syrup and are cold.

SERVING SUGGESTION:

Serve at tea with gulab jamun, pakora, samosa and chutney.

DALMOD

BOMBAY MIX

MAKES: 1 MEDIUM TIN

*D*almod is a beautiful combination of several nuts, lentils, rice flakes, sev etc. It is an excellent accompaniment for drinks. Dalmod is consumed not only as a day-to-day snack, but is also served during parties.

PREPARING THE SEV:

INGREDIENTS:	METRIC	IMPERIAL	AMERICAN
Gram flour, sifted	150 g	5 oz	$^2/_3$ cup
Oil	10 ml	2 tsp	2 tsp
Garam masala	2.5 ml	$^1/_2$ tsp	$^1/_2$ tsp
Ground red chilli	2.5 ml	$^1/_2$ tsp	$^1/_2$ tsp
Tymol seeds (ajwain)	2.5 ml	$^1/_2$ tsp	$^1/_2$ tsp
Salt to taste			
Water, lukewarm	100 ml	$3^1/_2$ fl oz	$6^1/_2$ tbsp
Oil for frying			

COOKING TIME: 50 MINUTES

1 Place the sifted flour in a bowl.

2 Rub in the oil, then mix in the above spices and salt thoroughly. Gradually pour in the water to make a thick, smooth batter.

3 Place the oil in a deep frying pan (skillet) on medium heat. Place a small thread nozzle on the sev machine and fill to three-quarters full with the batter.

4 Hold the machine above the hot oil, slowly press the handle or turn it round (depending upon the type of machine you have), swiftly moving the hand holding the machine in a circle and let the batter fall in long strips – do not overlap the strips.

5 Fry until light golden brown. Remove with a slotted spoon and leave to cool. Break into 2.5 cm/ 1 in pieces.

STEP 9

PREPARING THE CHEVDA:

Pawa (flaked rice)	100 g	4 oz	1 cup
Oil for frying			

Heat the oil in a deep frying pan (skillet) on high heat. Place a handful of pawa into the hot oil. Immediately turn them over and take them out (reduce the heat to low while taking them out, heat your oil again on high heat before frying more pawa).

PREPARING THE CHICKPEAS OR LENTILS:

Chickpeas/garbanzos, cleaned, soaked overnight, washed and dried completely	100 g	4 oz	²/₃ cup
Oil for frying			

Heat the oil in a deep frying pan (skillet) on high heat. Fry the chickpeas until crispy and golden brown. Chickpeas tend to pop, so do cover a little while frying.

PREPARING THE KAJU (CASHEW-NUTS):

Cashew-nuts	100 g	4 oz	1 cup
Oil for frying			

Heat the oil in a deep frying pan (skillet) on medium-low heat and fry the nuts until light golden brown.

PREPARING THE MOONGPHALI (PEANUTS):

Fresh shelled nuts	150 g	5 oz	²/₃ cup
Oil for frying			

Heat the oil in a deep frying pan (skillet) on medium heat and fry the peanuts until crispy golden brown.

TARKA:

Oil	15 ml	1 tbsp	1 tbsp
Mustard seeds	5 ml	1 tsp	1 tsp
Garam masala	5 ml	1 tsp	1 tsp
Ground roasted cumin	5 ml	1 tsp	1 tsp

Aniseed	15 ml	1 tbsp	1 tbsp
Ground red chilli	2.5 ml	½ tsp	½ tsp
Salt to taste			
Raisins	150 g	5 oz	5 oz
Sugar	15 ml	1 tbsp	1 tbsp
Citric acid	5 ml	1 tsp	1 tsp

1 Heat the oil in a large heavy-bottomed saucepan. Add the mustard seeds, then when they start crackling stir in all the ground spices (garam masala, cumin, aniseed, red chilli), salt and the raisins.

2 Turn the heat off. When still slightly hot mix in the sugar and the citric acid. Add fried sev, chevda, chickpeas, kaju and moongphali in tarka. If the saucepan is not large enough, place everything in a large bowl. Mix it thoroughly.

TO PRESERVE:

When cold keep it in an airtight container. It will keep over a fortnight.

SERVING SUGGESTION:

Serve at tea or as a nibble with drinks.

M enus from both the south and the north of India are included in this step. Onion Paratha is very quick and easy to make. Many Indians take this bread to school or work to give them a nourishing and filling lunch. Usually it is eaten with pickle/plain natural yoghurt/sabji (a vegetable dish such as okra, bitter gourd, cauliflower and potato) and Urud Dal. The method of cooking Urud Ki Sukhi Dal in this book is Punjabi style and this is one of my father's favourite dishes.

ONION PARATHA

HOT ONION BREAD

MAKES 12

O nion Paratha is one of the simplest parathas to make and it is one of Indian children's packed lunch items. Chop the onion very finely, otherwise it will be difficult to roll.

INGREDIENTS:	METRIC	IMPERIAL	AMERICAN
Brown chapati flour	525 g	1 lb 3 oz	4¾ cups
Medium onion, finely chopped	1	1	1
Small green chilli, finely chopped	1	1	1
Green coriander/cilantro leaves, chopped	30 ml	2 tbsp	2 tbsp
Oil	15 ml	1 tbsp	1 tbsp
Garam masala	5 ml	1 tsp	1 tsp
Tymol seeds (ajwain)	5 ml	1 tsp	1 tsp
Ground red chilli	2.5 ml	½ tsp	½ tsp
Salt to taste			
Water, lukewarm	250 ml	9 fl oz	1 cup

Place all the above ingredients into a large bowl with 500 g/1 lb 2 oz/4½ cups flour (keep the rest of the flour for rolling) and mix well. Pour in the water and make a soft dough. Knead it for 5 minutes or until the dough is springy and satiny. Cover and leave for 20 minutes.

Butter or ghee to smear	
Oil for frying	

COOKING TIME: 40 MINUTES

1 Heat a flat frying pan (skillet) on a medium heat. While the frying pan is heating, divide the dough into 12 equal portions.

2 Take a portion of dough and roll it into a ball on the palms of your hands. Dust it with flour, flatten it and roll into a small circle. Smear half with 2.5 ml/½ tsp ghee or butter and fold it in half. Smear the half again with ghee and fold again (one should now have a triangle).

3 Roll out again with the help of a little dry flour to 3 mm/⅛ in thick (keeping the triangular shape).

4 Place the onion paratha on the hot pan and cook both sides dry like a chapati. Then pour 7.5 ml/½ tbsp oil over it, fry the first side until light brown. Make 6 or 7 small slits on the paratha. Pour another 7.5 ml/½ tbsp oil and fry the other side light golden brown as well.

SERVING SUGGESTION:

Serve hot with pickle, butter, natural yoghurt, fried okra, urud ki sukhi dal and an aubergine/eggplant dish.

ALOO, GOBHI AND GOSHT

POTATO, CAULIFLOWER AND MEAT CURRY

SERVES: 4–6

T his is a lovely meat dish with vegetables. One can add a vegetable according to one's taste. This is a medium-hot dish.

INGREDIENTS:	METRIC	IMPERIAL	AMERICAN
Oil for frying			
Cauliflower, cut into 2.5 cm/ 1 in florets	250 g	9 oz	1¼ cups
Potatoes peeled, cut into 2.5 cm/ 1 in pieces	150 g	5 oz	1¼ cups

Heat the oil in a deep frying pan (skillet) on medium heat and fry the cauliflower and potato pieces until they are golden brown. Place them on a cooling tray and set them to one side.

Oil or ghee	75 ml	5 tbsp	5 tbsp
Mustard seeds	5 ml	1 tsp	1 tsp
Cumin seeds	5 ml	1 tsp	1 tsp
Large garlic cloves, crushed	5	5	5
Fresh ginger, finely chopped	4 cm	1½ in	1½ in
Medium onions, finely chopped	2	2	2
*Peppercorns	6	6	6
*Cloves	4	4	4
*Cinnamon stick	2.5 cm	1 in	1 in
Bay leaves	2	2	2
*Black cardamom	1	1	1
Meat, boned, cut into 2.5 cm/ 1 in pieces, fat trimmed off and washed	500 g	1 lb 2 oz	4½ cups
Ground coriander/cilantro	10 ml	2 tsp	2 tsp

Garam masala	5 ml	1 tsp	1 tsp
Ground turmeric	2.5 ml	$\frac{1}{2}$ tsp	$\frac{1}{2}$ tsp
Ground red chilli	2.5 ml	$\frac{1}{2}$ tsp	$\frac{1}{2}$ tsp
Tomatoes, tinned	400 g	14 oz	2 cups
Salt to taste			

TO GARNISH:

Garam masala	2.5 ml	$\frac{1}{2}$ tsp	$\frac{1}{2}$ tsp
Green coriander/cilantro leaves, chopped	15 ml	1 tbsp	1 tbsp
Small green chilli, chopped	1	1	1

COOKING TIME: 35 MINUTES

1 Heat the oil in a large heavy-bottomed saucepan on medium heat. Add the mustard seeds and when they start crackling brown the cumin seeds.

2 Put in the garlic, ginger, onions, peppercorns, cloves, cinnamon, bay leaves and black cardamom and fry gently until golden brown.

3 Add the meat pieces and fry for 5 minutes.

4 Stir in the coriander, garam masala, turmeric, red chilli, tomatoes and salt, and cook until all the liquid has been absorbed.

5 Pour in 50 ml/2 fl oz/3½ tbsp water and cook until all the water is absorbed. Put in 120 ml/4 fl oz/½ cup water. Reduce the heat to low, close the lid and simmer until the meat is tender.

6 Mix in the fried vegetables and cook on a low heat for a further 5 minutes.

7 Sprinkle over the garnish before serving.

SERVING SUGGESTION:

Serve hot with chapati, rice, rayta and dal.

MIXED VEGETABLE KORMA

SERVES: 4–6

This delightfully refreshing dish has a distinct flavour of coconut, fenugreek seeds, tamarind, spices and vegetables. This is a medium-hot recipe though south Indians generally make their dishes very hot.

INGREDIENTS:	METRIC	IMPERIAL	AMERICAN
Oil	75 ml	5 tbsp	5 tbsp
Fenugreek seeds	5 ml	1 tsp	1 tsp
Mustard seeds	5 ml	1 tsp	1 tsp
Large garlic cloves	3	3	3
Fresh ginger, finely chopped	2.5 cm	1 in	1 in
Medium onion, finely chopped	1	1	1
Coconut, desiccated, ground in a grinder	90 ml	6 tbsp	6 tbsp
Garam masala	5 ml	1 tsp	1 tsp
Ground coriander/cilantro	5 ml	1 tsp	1 tsp
Ground roasted cumin	5 ml	1 tsp	1 tsp
Ground red chilli	2.5 ml	$\frac{1}{2}$ tsp	$\frac{1}{2}$ tsp
Ground turmeric	2.5 ml	$\frac{1}{2}$ tsp	$\frac{1}{2}$ tsp
Salt to taste			
Tomatoes, tinned	400 g	14 oz	$1\frac{3}{4}$ cups
Tamarind, pulp extracted (see page 24)	50 g	2 oz	$\frac{1}{4}$ cup
Small cauliflower, split into 2.5 cm/1 in florets and washed	1	1	1
Small carrots, peeled, washed and cut into 4 cm/$1\frac{1}{2}$ in pieces	6	6	6
Water	400 ml	14 fl oz	2 cups
Medium aubergine/eggplant, washed, quartered and cut into 1.2 cm/$\frac{1}{2}$ in pieces	1	1	1
Medium green/bell pepper, washed, quartered and cut into 1.2 cm/$\frac{1}{2}$ in pieces	1	1	1

Medium potato, peeled, washed and cut into 1 cm/½ in pieces	1	1	1

TO GARNISH:

Garam masala	2.5 ml	½ tsp	½ tsp
Green coriander/cilantro, leaves, chopped	15 ml	1 tbsp	1 tbsp
Small green chilli, chopped	1	1	1

COOKING TIME: 1 HOUR

1 Heat the oil in a large heavy-bottomed saucepan and brown the fenugreek and mustard seeds. Add the garlic, ginger and onion and fry until golden brown. Add coconut and fry for a further 2 minutes.

2 Mix in the garam masala, coriander, roasted cumin, red chilli, turmeric and salt, then the tomatoes and cook until all the liquid has been absorbed and the oil appears on the surface of the mixture.

3 Put in the cauliflower, carrot and 250 ml/8 fl oz/ 1 cup water. Bring to the boil. Reduce the heat to medium-low and cook for 15 minutes. Add the aubergine, green pepper, potato and the rest of the water and the tamarind pulp and cook for a further 30 minutes or until the vegetables are tender.

4 Sprinkle over the garnish before serving.

SERVING SUGGESTION:

Serve hot with idli or puri, yoghurt, rice and dal.

URUD
KI SUKHI DAL

WHITE SPLIT URUD LENTIL

SERVES: 4–6

Urud dal is not easy to digest, therefore we must add asafoetida, ginger and garlic. This dish is medium-hot.

INGREDIENTS:	METRIC	IMPERIAL	AMERICAN
Urud dal, cleaned and washed	350 g	12 oz	2 cups
Ground turmeric	2.5 ml	$\frac{1}{2}$ tsp	$\frac{1}{2}$ tsp
Salt to taste			
Water	750 ml	$1\frac{1}{4}$ cups	3 cups

TARKA:

Ghee or oil	60 ml	4 tbsp	4 tbsp
Large pinch of asafoetida			
Large garlic cloves, crushed	3	3	3
Fresh ginger, chopped	2.5 cm	1 in	1 in
Large onion, finely chopped	1	1	1
Ground red chilli	2.5 ml	$\frac{1}{2}$ tsp	$\frac{1}{2}$ tsp
Ground turmeric	1.5 ml	$\frac{1}{4}$ tsp	$\frac{1}{4}$ tsp
Garam masala	2.5 ml	$\frac{1}{2}$ tsp	$\frac{1}{2}$ tsp
Ground roasted cumin	5 ml	1 tsp	1 tsp

TO GARNISH:

Green coriander/cilantro leaves, chopped	15 ml	1 tbsp	1 tbsp
Garam masala	2.5 ml	$\frac{1}{2}$ tsp	$\frac{1}{2}$ tsp
Small green chilli	1	1	1
Lemon, cut into small pieces	1	1	1

128

COOKING TIME: 50 MINUTES

1 Place the washed lentils, turmeric, salt and the water into a large saucepan. Bring to the boil, skim off any scum and simmer on a low heat for 45 minutes or until the dal is tender.

2 If any water is left, dry it off on a high heat but don't stir, otherwise the dal will become mushy.

3 While the dal is cooking, prepare the tarka. Heat the ghee or oil in a heavy-bottomed saucepan. Add the asafoetida, garlic, ginger and the onion and fry gently on a medium heat until they are golden brown.

4 Add the red chilli, turmeric, garam masala and roasted cumin, and remove the pan from the heat and set it to one side.

5 Stir in the cooked dal.

6 Sprinkle over the garnish before serving.

SERVING SUGGESTION:

Serve hot with chapati or onion paratha, karela (bitter gourd), stuffed aubergine/eggplant, gajar-matar ki sabji (carrot and peas curry), potato curry and rayta.

V

HOT FRIED CAULIFLOWER

SERVES:4–6

This is a very simple way of cooking cauliflower and it is very delicious too. You'll find this dish to be medium-hot.

INGREDIENTS:	METRIC	IMPERIAL	AMERICAN
Large cauliflower, cut into 12 florets, the stems peeled thinly and cut into 5 mm/¼ in thick rounds and washed	1	1	1
Oil for frying			

Place the oil in a deep frying pan (skillet) on a medium heat and fry the cauliflower until lightly golden brown.

	METRIC	IMPERIAL	AMERICAN
Oil or ghee	30 ml	2 tbsp	2 tbsp
Mustard seeds	5 ml	1 tsp	1 tsp
Onion seeds (kalonji)	5 ml	1 tsp	1 tsp
Cumin seeds	5 ml	1 tsp	1 tsp
Ground coriander/cilantro	5 ml	1 tsp	1 tsp
Garam masala	5 ml	1 tsp	1 tsp
Ground roasted cumin	5 ml	1 tsp	1 tsp
Ground ginger	2.5 ml	½ tsp	½ tsp
Ground red chilli	2.5 ml	½ tsp	½ tsp
Ground turmeric	2.5 ml	½ tsp	½ tsp
Sugar	15 ml	1 tbsp	1 tbsp
Lemon juice	30 ml	2 tbsp	2 tbsp
Salt to taste			

TO GARNISH:

	METRIC	IMPERIAL	AMERICAN
Garam masala	2.5 ml	½ tsp	½ tsp
Green coriander/cilantro leaves, chopped	15 ml	1 tbsp	1 tbsp
Small green chilli, chopped	1	1	1

COOKING TIME: 15 MINUTES

1 Heat the oil or ghee in a large heavy-bottomed saucepan on a medium heat.

2 Add the mustard seeds and the onion seeds and when the mustard seeds start crackling brown the cumin seeds.

3 Stir in the ground spices and the cauliflower.

4 Reduce the heat to low and cook for 10 minutes.

5 Mix in the sugar and the lemon juice and cook for a further 2 minutes. Add the salt.

6 Sprinkle over the garnish before serving.

SERVING SUGGESTION:

Serve hot with puri, dal, rayta and biryani.

In India we make paneer (Indian-style cheese) at home. When it is cooked it becomes even more soft and spongy. Matar Paneer is often served during weddings or parties. Chicken Mughlai Biryani is another royal dish which is liked by all my cookery class pupils. Two more side dishes are also included, Kala Channa and another rayta.
Tirangi Barfi is a sweet which can be consumed after a meal or at tea-time as a snack. It looks beautiful and tastes delicious.

MATAR PANEER

PEAS AND INDIAN CHEESE

SERVES: 4–6

This dish is thoroughly enjoyed by both non-vegetarians and vegetarians. The paneer is very rich in protein. You will find this dish to be medium-hot.

INGREDIENTS:	METRIC	IMPERIAL	AMERICAN
Large garlic cloves	3	3	3
Fresh ginger	2.5 cm	1 in	1 in
Medium onion, cut into large pieces	1	1	1

Combine the garlic, ginger and onion in a blender and blend with 45 ml/3 tbsp water to make a smooth paste.

Paneer (see page 23)	2.25 litres	4 pts	10 cups
Oil for frying			
Ghee or oil	60 ml	4 tbsp	4 tbsp
Cumin seeds	5 ml	1 tsp	1 tsp
Small onion, finely chopped	1	1	1
*Cloves	4	4	4
*Peppercorns	4	4	4
Bay leaves	2	2	2
*Black cardamom	1	1	1
*Cinnamon	2.5 cm	1 in	1 in
Ground coriander/cilantro	10 ml	2 tsp	2 tsp
Garam masala	5 ml	1 tsp	1 tsp
Ground red chilli	2.5 ml	$^1/_2$ tsp	$^1/_2$ tsp
Ground turmeric	2.5 ml	$^1/_2$ tsp	$^1/_2$ tsp
Salt to taste			
Tomatoes, tinned	400 g	14 oz	$1^3/_4$ cups
Whey water (from paneer)	600 ml	1 pt	$2^1/_2$ cups
Peas, frozen, or fresh, shelled	500 g	1 lb 2 oz	$4^1/_2$ cups

TO GARNISH:

Garam masala	2.5 ml	¹/₂ tsp	¹/₂ tsp
Green coriander/cilantro leaves, chopped	15 ml	1 tbsp	1 tbsp
Small green chilli, chopped	1	1	1

COOKING TIME: 50 MINUTES

1 Chop the paneer into 1.2 cm/½ in cubes and deep-fry in oil until light brown, take them out with a slotted spoon and set them to one side.

2 Heat the ghee or oil in a large heavy-bottomed saucepan. Add the cumin seeds and brown them.

3 Put in the chopped onion and whole spices, fry until golden brown.

4 Stir in the blended paste and fry for a further few minutes until golden brown.

5 Add the coriander, garam masala, red chilli, turmeric, salt and tomatoes and cook on medium heat until all the liquid has been absorbed.

6 Pour 60 ml/4 tbsp whey water into the pan and fry until all the water has been absorbed and the ghee appears on the surface of the mixture.

7 Add rest of the whey water, fresh peas and the fried paneer pieces and simmer for 15 minutes until the peas are cooked and paneer is soft and spongy. (If using the frozen peas, simmer for only 5 minutes and add only 300 ml/½ pint/1¼ cups whey water.)

8 Sprinkle over the garnish before serving.

SERVING SUGGESTION:

Serve hot with puri, pulao, cauliflower, dal and a chicken curry.

CHICKEN MUGHLAI BIRYANI

SERVES: 4

The Mughal introduced a lot of lavish dishes to Indian cuisine. These are more popular in north India and Muslim houses. This rice dish is delicate and delicious, and is best eaten the moment it is prepared. You will find this dish to be medium-hot.

PREPARING THE CHICKEN:

INGREDIENTS:	METRIC	IMPERIAL	AMERICAN
Natural yoghurt	150 ml	1/4 pt	2/3 cup
Large garlic cloves	3	3	3
Fresh ginger	2.5 cm	1 in	1 in
Chicken (leg and breast), skinned, washed and cut into 2.5 cm/1 in pieces	500 g	1 lb 2 oz	18 oz

Combine the yoghurt, cloves and ginger in a blender and blend to make a smooth paste. Place it in a bowl. Add the chicken pieces and marinate for two hours.

Oil	90 ml	6 tbsp	6 tbsp
Small onions, thinly sliced	5	5	5

Heat the oil in a saucepan on medium heat and fry the onions gently until golden brown. Take out the onions with a slotted spoon and set on one side.

Oil	75 ml	5 tbsp	5 tbsp
Cumin seeds	5 ml	1 tsp	1 tsp
Bay leaves	2	2	2
Garam masala	5 ml	1 tsp	1 tsp
Ground coriander/cilantro	5 ml	1 tsp	1 tsp
Ground red chilli	2.5 ml	1/2 tsp	1/2 tsp
Ground turmeric	2.5 ml	1/2 tsp	1/2 tsp
Salt to taste			
Tomatoes, tinned	225 g	8 oz	1 cup

CHICKEN MUGHLAI BIRYANI

STEP 11

Coriander/cilantro leaves, chopped	30 ml	2 tbsp	2 tbsp
Green chilli, chopped	1	1	1

COOKING TIME: 30 MINUTES

1 Heat the oil in a saucepan and brown the cumin seeds and bay leaves on medium heat.

2 Add the chicken pieces only and fry for 5 minutes.

3 Gradually pour in the rest of the marinade and cook until all the liquid has been absorbed.

4 Stir in the garam masala, coriander, red chilli, turmeric, salt and then the tomatoes. Cook until all the liquid is absorbed and the oil appears on the surface of the mixture.

5 Pour in 100 ml/3½ fl oz 6½ tbsp water. Bring to the boil. Reduce the heat to low. Close the lid and simmer for 15 minutes or until the chicken is tender and all the liquid has been absorbed, stirring a few times.

6 While the chicken is cooking prepare the rice.

7 Mix in the coriander leaves and green chilli before putting the cooked chicken in layers.

PREPARING THE RICE:

Ghee	45 ml	3 tbsp	3 tbsp
Cumin seeds	5 ml	1 tsp	1 tsp
Bay leaves	3	3	3
Rice (patna or basmati), cleaned, washed and drained	150 g	5 oz	1 cup
Garam masala	5 ml	1 tsp	1 tsp
Ground nutmeg	1.5 ml	¼ tsp	¼ tsp
Ground mace	1.5 ml	¼ tsp	¼ tsp
Salt to taste			
Raisins	100 g	4 oz	⅔ cup
Almonds, blanched and cut in halves lengthwise	50 g	2 oz	½ cup

Cashew-nuts, cut in halves lengthwise	50 g	2 oz	1/2 cup
Water	300 ml	1/2 pt	1 1/4 cups
Milk, warm	50 ml	2 fl oz	1/4 cup
Saffron	1.5 ml	1/4 tsp	1/4 tsp

COOKING TIME: 15 MINUTES

1 Heat the ghee in a saucepan and brown the cumin seeds and the bay leaves.

2 Add the rice and fry for 2 minutes on medium heat.

3 Stir in the garam masala, nutmeg, mace, salt, raisins, almonds and cashew-nuts.

4 Pour in the water and mix thoroughly. Bring to the boil, close the lid, reduce the heat to low and simmer for 10 minutes.

5 Turn off the heat and leave for 5 minutes.

6 Place the milk and saffron in a cup for at least a few minutes.

LAYERING THE CHICKEN AND RICE:

1 In a heavy-bottomed saucepan, put layers of chicken, fried onion and then rice. Repeat until all the ingredients are used up.

2 Sprinkle over the saffron milk. Close the lid and cook for 2–3 minutes on low heat. Turn the heat off and leave for 5 minutes.

3 Open the lid, place a flat serving dish over the saucepan and turn over. Tap the saucepan with a large spoon. Lift the pan up, making sure all the biryani is on the serving dish.

SERVING SUGGESTION:

Serve hot with puri or chapati, rayta, dal and pumpkin kofta curry.

DHANIVA PUDEENA KA RAYTA

CORIANDER AND MINT IN YOGHURT

SERVES 4–6

This is another rayta which is very refreshing, delicious and easy to make.

INGREDIENTS:	METRIC	IMPERIAL	AMERICAN
Natural yoghurt, chilled and whisked until smooth	450 ml	¾ pt	2 cups
Fresh coriander/cilantro, finely chopped	30 ml	2 tbsp	2 tbsp
Fresh mint, finely chopped	30 ml	2 tbsp	2 tbsp
Dried mint OR roasted cumin	5 ml	1 tsp	1 tsp
Small green chilli, finely chopped	1	1	1
Salt to taste			

1 Place the whisked yoghurt in a deep bowl.

2 Mix all the above ingredients thoroughly.

SERVING SUGGESTION:

Serve chilled with any meal.

✳ KALA CHANNA

WHOLE BLACK GRAM

SERVES: 4

I vividly remember my late mother saying, 'If you eat kala channa you'll be as strong as a horse'. In our school once a week all children up to the age of 16 years used to get kala channa. Other days we used to get a banana, or guava or puffed rice etc. The kala channa was either roasted, or as prepared in the recipe below. You'll find this dish to be medium-hot.

INGREDIENTS:	METRIC	IMPERIAL	AMERICAN
Kala channa, soaked overnight, cleaned and washed	250 g	9 oz	2¼ cups
Salt to taste			
Water	600 ml	1 pt	2½ cups
Oil	30 ml	2 tbsp	2 tbsp
Cumin seeds	5 ml	1 tsp	1 tsp
Ground coriander/cilantro	5 ml	1 tsp	1 tsp
Garam masala	5 ml	1 tsp	1 tsp
Ground red chilli	2.5 ml	½ tsp	½ tsp
Roasted cumin	5 ml	1 tsp	1 tsp
Amchoor (dry ground mango)	30 ml	2 tbsp	2 tbsp
OR lemon juice	60 ml	4 tbsp	4 tbsp

TO GARNISH:

Medium tomato, finely chopped	1	1	1
Small onion, finely chopped	1	1	1
Green coriander/cilantro leaves, chopped	15 ml	1 tbsp	1 tbsp
Green chilli, finely chopped	1	1	1

COOKING TIME: 40 MINUTES

1 Place the kala channa, salt and water in a large saucepan on a high heat. Bring it to boil, skim off any scum and simmer over medium heat for 30 minutes or until the kala channa are tender.

2 Heat the oil in a heavy-based pan and fry the cumin seeds until lightly brown.

3 Stir in the ground spices, kala channa and amchoor or lemon juice.

4 Simmer over medium heat for a further 5–6 minutes or until all the liquid has been absorbed.

5 Sprinkle over the garnish ingredients

SERVING SUGGESTION:

Eat hot or cold on its own as a snack or during meal with puri, pumpkin and carrot halwa.

TIRANGI BARFI

THREE-COLOURED BARFI

MAKES: 22

*I*ndia got her independence on 15 August 1947 and this *auspicious day is celebrated throughout India. The Indian Tirangi (yellow, white and green) flag is waved everywhere. Tirangi barfis are distributed in schools and the shelves in sweetshops are decorated with them.*

PREPARING THE FIRST LAYER (BOTTOM):

INGREDIENTS:	METRIC	IMPERIAL	AMERICAN
Full cream milk powder	50 g	2 oz	$^1/_2$ cup
Double (heavy) cream, whipped	60 ml	4 tbsp	4 tbsp
Ghee, melted	10 ml	2 tsp	2 tsp
Pistachios, coarsely ground in a coffee grinder	25 g	1 oz	2 tbsp
Sugar	25 g	1 oz	2 tbsp
Water	25 ml	1 fl oz	$1^1/_2$ tbsp
Food colour, green	2.5 ml	$^1/_2$ tsp	$^1/_2$ tsp
Essence: kevera or gulab water	2.5 ml	$^1/_2$ tsp	$^1/_2$ tsp

TOTAL COOKING TIME: 25 MINUTES

1 Place the milk powder and cream in a bowl with 5 ml/1 tsp of the ghee and mix thoroughly. Set the bowl on one side.

2 Place the pistachios and the remaining ghee in a saucepan on a medium-low heat and fry for 3 minutes or until light brown. Add this to the milk powder mixture.

3 Place the sugar, water and food colour in the same saucepan on a medium heat.

4 Boil it until it is ready to set. (Test by letting a drop of syrup fall into a cup of cold water, if the drop sets and stays at the bottom it is ready.)

STEP 11

5 Stir in the milk powder mixture and the essence. Mix thoroughly until it is smooth and a little cool. Spread on a greased plate and shape into a square about 1.2 cm/½ in thick.

PREPARING THE SECOND LAYER (MIDDLE):

Full cream milk powder	50 g	2 oz	½ cup
Double (heavy) cream, whipped	60 ml	4 tbsp	4 tbsp
Ghee, melted	10 ml	2 tsp	2 tsp
Almonds, blanched, dried and coarsely ground in a coffee grinder	25 g	1 oz	2 tbsp
Sugar	25 g	1 oz	2 tbsp
Water	25 ml	1 fl oz	1½ tbsp

1 Place the milk powder and cream in a bowl with 5 ml/1 tsp of the ghee and mix thoroughly. Set the bowl on one side.

2 Place the almonds and the remaining ghee in a saucepan on a medium-low heat and fry for 3 minutes or until light brown. Add this to the milk powder mixture.

3 Place the sugar, and the water in the same saucepan on a medium heat.

4 Boil it until it is ready to set.

5 Stir in the milk powder mixture. Mix thoroughly until it is smooth and a little cool. Spread it over the first layer about 1.2 cm/½ in thick.

PREPARING THE THIRD LAYER (TOP):

Full cream milk powder	50 g	2 oz	½ cup
Double (heavy) cream, whipped	60 ml	4 tbsp	4 tbsp
Ground green cardamom	5 ml	1 tsp	1 tsp
Ghee, melted	10 ml	2 tsp	2 tsp
Coconut, desiccated	25 g	1 oz	2 tbsp
Sugar	25 g	1 oz	2 tbsp
Water	25 ml	1 fl oz	1 fl oz
Food colour, yellow	2.5 ml	½ tsp	½ tsp

Saffron	1.5 ml	$\frac{1}{4}$ tsp	$\frac{1}{4}$ tsp
Varak (fine, edible silver sheet) (optional)	1	1	1

1 Place the milk powder, cream and half the cardamom in a bowl with 5 ml/1 tsp of the ghee and mix thoroughly. Set the bowl on one side.

2 Place the coconut and remaining ghee in a saucepan on a medium-low heat and fry for 3 minutes or until light brown. Add this to the milk powder mixture.

3 Place the sugar, water, the remaining ground green cardamom, the colour and the saffron in the same saucepan on medium heat.

4 Boil it until it is ready to set

5 Stir in the milk powder mixture. Mix thoroughly until it is smooth and a little cool. Spread it over the second layer about 1.2 cm/½ in thick.

6 Cover with varak, if using, and leave to set in a cool place for 3–4 hours.

7 Cut into squares or triangles.

SERVING SUGGESTION:

Serve cold after a meal or at tea.

STEP 12

Over the last few years Sweet and Sour Prawns has become increasingly popular in India, along with Sweet and Sour Vegetables. For this reason I felt I should introduce it in this book. The sauce can be used as a dip. Vegetarians and non-vegetarians will both enjoy the aubergine and potato dish. Stuffed Aloo Paratha with pickle is also used for packed lunches and breakfast. It is quite amusing to see (if you get a chance to go to India) how many people will without fail eat an aloo paratha when travelling anywhere by train.

Dhandai is a cold milk drink with nuts. This is considered to be very healthy and whoever can afford the drink has it in both hot and cold weather.

SWEET AND SOUR PRAWNS

SERVES: 4–5

*T*his is another popular dish with my parents and
brothers. The subtle blend of spices, honey and vinegar
makes this recipe easily adaptable to suit other meats e.g.
pork or chicken. (Sweet and sour chicken can be prepared
simply by substituting the prawns with small pre-cooked
chicken pieces.) You will find this dish to be medium-hot.

BATTER:

INGREDIENTS:	METRIC	IMPERIAL	AMERICAN
Gram flour, sifted	100 g	4 oz	1 cup
Oil	15 ml	1 tbsp	1 tbsp
Green coriander/cilantro leaves, chopped	15 ml	1 tbsp	1 tbsp
Ground red chilli	2.5 ml	$\frac{1}{2}$ tsp	$\frac{1}{2}$ tsp
Green chilli, chopped	1	1	1
Garam masala	5 ml	1 tsp	1 tsp
Salt to taste			
Tymol seeds (ajwain)	5 ml	1 tbsp	1 tbsp
Water, warm	150 ml	$\frac{1}{4}$ pt	$\frac{2}{3}$ cup

1 Place the sifted flour in a bowl and mix in the oil.

2 Add the coriander leaves, green and red chilli,
garam masala, salt and tymol seeds.

3 Pour in the water to make a smooth batter.

Oil for frying			
Prawns (shrimp), cooked, shelled and washed	125 g	$4\frac{1}{2}$ oz	$4\frac{1}{2}$ oz
Vegetables: cauliflower, carrots, green pepper, aubergine/eggplant or any other, washed and cut into 4 cm/$1\frac{1}{2}$ in pieces.	250 g	9 oz	$2\frac{1}{2}$ cups

FRYING TIME: 30 MINUTES

1 Heat the oil in a deep frying pan (skillet) on medium heat.

2 Dip each cooked prawn piece in the batter and place gently in the hot oil.

3 Fry all the prawn pieces together until golden brown.

4 Remove the prawns with a slotted spoon and put them in a serving dish.

5 Now dip the vegetable pieces in the batter and fry 7–8 pieces together until golden brown.

6 Place them with the prawn pieces in the serving dish and set on one side.

SAUCE:

Large garlic cloves	4	4	4
Fresh ginger, coarsely chopped	2.5 cm	1 in	1 in
Medium onion, coarsely chopped	1	1	1

Combine the garlic, ginger and onion in a blender and blend to make a smooth paste.

Oil or ghee	75 ml	5 tbsp	5 tbsp
Small onion, finely chopped	1	1	1
Garam masala	5 ml	1 tsp	1 tsp
Ground coriander/cilantro	10 ml	2 tsp	2 tsp
Ground red chilli	2.5 ml	1/2 tsp	1/2 tsp
Ground turmeric	2.5 ml	1/2 tsp	1/2 tsp
Salt to taste italic			
Ground nutmeg	1.5 ml	1/4 tsp	1/4 tsp
Ground mace	1.5 ml	1/4 tsp	1/4 tsp
Ground roasted cumin	5 ml	1 tsp	1 tsp
Tomatoes, tinned	230 g	8 oz	1 3/4 cups
Vinegar	60 ml	4 tbsp	4 tbsp
Honey	15 ml	1 tbsp	1 tbsp
Water	200 ml	7 fl oz	scant 1 cup

TO GARNISH:

Garam masala	2.5 ml	½ tsp	½ tsp
Green coriander/cilantro leaves, chopped	15 ml	1 tbsp	1 tbsp
Small green chilli, chopped	1	1	1

COOKING TIME: 30 MINUTES

1 Heat the ghee in a heavy-bottomed saucepan and fry gently the chopped onions until golden brown.

2 Add the blended paste and fry until golden brown.

3 Put in garam masala, coriander, red chilli, turmeric, salt, nutmeg, mace, roasted cumin and the tomatoes.

4 Cook until all the liquid has been absorbed and the ghee appears on the surface of the mixture.

5 Pour in the vinegar and cook until all the liquid is absorbed.

6 Add the honey and cook for a further 2 minutes.

7 Finally add the water and bring to the boil.

8 Reduce the heat to low and simmer for 2 minutes.

9 Pour the hot sauce over the fried prawns and vegetable pieces just before you want to serve and sprinkle over the garnish.

SERVING SUGGESTION:

Serve hot with rice, puri, rayta and chutney.

AUBERGINE AND POTATO

WEST INDIAN GUJRATI STYLE

SERVES: 4

*A*ubergines/eggplant grow in different shapes and sizes and Indians prepare different varieties of dishes with them. For this aubergine and potato dish, one needs a medium or large aubergine.

INGREDIENTS:	METRIC	IMPERIAL	AMERICAN
Oil	75 ml	5 tbsp	5 tbsp
Asafoetida	large pinch	$^1/_8$ tsp	$^1/_8$ tsp
Mustard seeds	2.5 ml	$^1/_2$ tsp	$^1/_2$ tsp
Fenugreek seeds	2.5 ml	$^1/_2$ tsp	$^1/_2$ tsp
Large garlic cloves, crushed	2	2	2
Small onion, finely chopped	1	1	1
Fresh ginger, finely chopped	1. 2 cm	$^1/_2$ in	$^1/_2$ in
Potatoes, peeled, washed and cut into 2.5 cm/1 in pieces	250 g	9 oz	$2^1/_4$ cups
Coconut, desiccated, or fresh, grated	15 ml	1 tbsp	1 tbsp
Aubergine/eggplant, washed and cut into 2.5 cm/1 in pieces	250 g	9 oz	$2^1/_4$ cups
Ground coriander/cilantro	5 ml	1 tsp	1 tsp
Ground roasted cumin	5 ml	1 tsp	1 tsp
Garam masala	2.5 ml	$^1/_2$ tsp	$^1/_2$ tsp
Ground red chilli	2.5 ml	$^1/_2$ tsp	$^1/_2$ tsp
Ground turmeric	2.5 ml	$^1/_2$ tsp	$^1/_2$ tsp
Salt to taste			
Tomatoes, tinned	230 g	8 oz	1 cup
Sugar (or jaggery)	15 ml	1 tbsp	1 tbsp
Lemon juice	15 ml	1 tbsp	1 tbsp

TO GARNISH:

Garam masala	1.5 ml	¼ tsp	¼ tsp
Green coriander/cilantro leaves, chopped	15 ml	1 tbsp	1 tbsp
Small green chilli, chopped	1	1	1

COOKING TIME: 35 MINUTES

1 Heat the oil in a large heavy-bottomed saucepan on a medium heat.

2 Add the asafoetida, mustard seeds and the fenugreek seeds and, when the mustard seeds start crackling, lightly brown the garlic, onion and the ginger.

3 Put in the potato pieces and fry until golden brown.

4 Mix in the coconut and the aubergine pieces and fry for 1 minute. Stir in the ground spices and then the tomatoes.

5 Reduce the heat to low, close the lid and cook for 20 minutes or until the vegetables are tender, stirring occasionally (if needed, add a little water).

6 Add the sugar and the lemon juice. Increase the heat and dry off any remaining liquid.

SERVING SUGGESTION:

Serve hot with dal, plain rice, rayta, chapati or paratha.

ALOO PARATHA

BREAD WITH POTATO STUFFING

MAKES: 11

This dish is often served at breakfast, and is delicious with natural yoghurt and pickle. This is also one of the breads which children take to school in their packed lunch boxes. You will find this recipe to be medium-hot.

PREPARING THE DOUGH:

INGREDIENTS:	METRIC	IMPERIAL	AMERICAN
Chapati flour, brown	275 g	10 oz	2$\frac{1}{2}$ cups
Oil	15 ml	1 tbsp	1 tbsp
Salt	1.5 ml	$\frac{1}{4}$ tsp	$\frac{1}{4}$ tsp
Water, lukewarm	150 ml	$\frac{1}{4}$ pt	$\frac{2}{3}$ cup

1 Place 250 g/9 oz/2$\frac{1}{4}$ cups flour into a bowl (keep the rest of the flour for rolling out). Rub the oil in it and add the salt.

2 Pour in the water to make a soft dough.

3 Knead it for 5 minutes or until the dough is soft, springy and satiny.

4 Cover and leave for 10 minutes.

PREPARING THE FILLING:

Potatoes, boiled in jackets, peeled and mashed	500 g	1 lb 2 oz	2$\frac{1}{4}$ cups
Green coriander/cilantro leaves, chopped	30 ml	2 tbsp	2 tbsp
Lemon juice (optional)	15 ml	1 tbsp	1 tbsp
Garam masala	5 ml	1 tsp	1 tsp
Ground red chilli	2.5 ml	$\frac{1}{2}$ tsp	$\frac{1}{2}$ tsp
Tymol seeds (ajwain)	2.5 ml	$\frac{1}{2}$ tsp	$\frac{1}{2}$ tsp
Fresh ginger, finely chopped	1.2 cm	$\frac{1}{2}$ in	$\frac{1}{2}$ in
Medium onion, finely chopped	1	1	1

Small green chilli, finely chopped	1	1	1
Salt to taste			

Place all the above ingredients into a bowl and mix thoroughly.

MAKING THE PARATHA:

Oil for frying

COOKING TIME: 35 MINUTES

1 Heat a flat frying pan (skillet) on medium heat.

2 While the frying pan is heating divide the dough into 11 equal portions.

3 Take a portion of dough and roll it into a ball on the palms of your hands.

4 Dust it with flour, flatten it and roll it into a small round shape.

5 Place 1 portion of filling on it and cover, bringing the edges together.

6 Again flatten, dust with flour and roll it into a round shape about 3 mm/⅛ in thick.

7 Place the aloo paratha on the hot pan and cook both sides 'dry' like a chapati.

8 Then pour 7.5 ml/½ tbsp oil over it and fry the first side until light golden brown. Make 6 or 7 slits in the paratha.

9 Pour in another 7.5 ml/½ tbsp oil and fry the other side until light golden brown as well.

SERVING SUGGESTION:

Serve hot with yoghurt, pickle and butter at breakfast. Take it on a picnic with stuffed aubergine, cauliflower or the pea-carrot dish, and natural yoghurt pickle.

SWEET AND SOUR VEGETABLES

SERVES 4–5

M y family all enjoy this dish. The subtle blend of spices, honey and vinegar makes this an easily adaptable recipe to most vegetables. You will find this dish to be medium-hot.

BATTER:

INGREDIENTS:	METRIC	IMPERIAL	AMERICAN
Gram flour, sifted	100 g	4 oz	$1\frac{1}{4}$ cup
Oil	15 ml	1 tbsp	1 tbsp
Green coriander/cilantro leaves, chopped	15 ml	1 tbsp	1 tbsp
Ground red chilli	2.5 ml	$\frac{1}{2}$ tsp	$\frac{1}{2}$ tsp
Green chilli, chopped	1	1	1
Garam masala	5 ml	1 tsp	1 tsp
Salt to taste			
Tymol seeds (ajwain)	5 ml	1 tsp	1 tsp
Water, warm	150 ml	5 fl oz	$\frac{2}{3}$ cup
Oil for frying			

1 Place the sifted flour in a bowl and mix in the oil.

2 Add the coriander leaves, green and red chilli, garam masala, salt, and tymol seeds.

3 Pour in the water to make a smooth batter.

Oil for frying			
Vegetables: cauliflower, carrots, green/bell pepper, aubergine/eggplant or any other, washed and cut into 4 cm/$1\frac{1}{2}$ in pieces.	400 g	14 oz	14 oz

FRYING TIME: 20 MINUTES

1 Heat the oil or ghee in a deep frying pan (skillet) on medium heat.

2 Dip the vegetable pieces in the batter and fry 7–8 pieces together until golden brown.

3 Place them in the serving dish and set on one side.

SAUCE:

Large garlic cloves	2	2	2
Fresh ginger, coarsely chopped	1.2 cm	$\frac{1}{2}$ in	$\frac{1}{2}$ in
Medium onion, coarsely chopped	1	1	1

Combine the garlic, ginger and onion in a blender and blend to make a smooth paste.

Oil or ghee	75 ml	5 tbsp	5 tbsp
Small onion, finely chopped	1	1	1
Garam masala	5 ml	1 tsp	1 tsp
Ground coriander/cilantro	10 ml	2 tsp	2 tsp
Ground red chilli	2.5 ml	$\frac{1}{2}$ tsp	$\frac{1}{2}$ tsp
Ground turmeric	2.5 ml	$\frac{1}{2}$ tsp	$\frac{1}{2}$ tsp
Salt to taste			
Ground nutmeg	1.25 ml	$\frac{1}{4}$ tsp	$\frac{1}{4}$ tsp
Ground mace	1.25 ml	$\frac{1}{4}$ tsp	$\frac{1}{4}$ tsp
Ground roasted cumin	5 ml	1 tsp	1 tsp
Tomatoes, tinned	220 g	8 oz	$1\frac{3}{4}$ cups
Vinegar	30 ml	2 tbsp	2 tbsp
Honey	15 ml	1 tbsp	1 tbsp
Water	200 ml	7 fl oz	1 cup

TO GARNISH:

Garam masala	2.5 ml	$\frac{1}{2}$ tsp	$\frac{1}{2}$ tsp
Green coriander/cilantro leaves, chopped	15 ml	1 tbsp	1 tbsp
Small green chilli, chopped	1	1	1

COOKING TIME: 30 MINUTES

1 Heat the oil or ghee in a heavy-bottomed saucepan and fry the chopped onion gently until golden brown.

2 Add the blended paste and fry until golden brown.

3 Add the garam masala, coriander, red chilli, turmeric, salt, nutmeg, mace, roasted cumin and the tomatoes.

4 Cook until all the liquid has been absorbed and the oil/ghee appears on the surface of the mixture.

5 Pour in the vinegar and cook until all the liquid is absorbed.

6 Add the honey and cook for a further 2 minutes.

7 Finally add the water and bring to the boil.

8 Reduce the heat to low and simmer for 2 minutes.

9 Pour the hot sauce over vegetable pieces just before you want to serve and sprinkle over the garnish; or dip your fried pieces in sauce while eating.

SERVING SUGGESTIONS:

Serve hot with rice, puri, rayta and chutney.

✳
DHANDAI

MAKES: 6 LARGE GLASSES

Holi is the Hindu's most exciting festival. It takes place in April to celebrate the victory of God and destruction of demons. People visit each other's homes to play with gulal (dry coloured powder with a sparkling substance in it) and to throw coloured water at each other. They sing and dance on their way between houses. The host graciously offers them lots of sweets and snacks to eat and 'dhandai' to drink.

INGREDIENTS:	METRIC	IMPERIAL	AMERICAN
Almonds, blanched	*25 g*	*1 oz*	*2 tbsp*
Pistachios	*15 g*	*½ oz*	*1 tbsp*
Milk	*1.2 litres*	*2 pts*	*5 cups*
Sugar	*50 g*	*2 oz*	*¼ cup*
Essence: kevera or gulab water	*5 ml*	*1 tsp*	*1 tsp*
Food colour, yellow (optional)	*2.5 ml*	*½ tsp*	*½ tsp*
Ground green cardamom	*1.5 ml*	*¼ tsp*	*¼ tsp*
Saffron	*1.5 ml*	*¼ tsp*	*¼ tsp*
Ground mace	*1.5 ml*	*¼ tsp*	*¼ tsp*
Ground nutmeg	*1.5 ml*	*¼ tsp*	*¼ tsp*
Ice			

1 Combine the almonds and pistachios in a coffee grinder and grind to a fine powder.

2 Pour the milk in a large jug. Add the sugar and mix until dissolved.

3 Stir in the rest of the ingredients.

SERVING SUGGESTION:

Serve cold instead of tea during the summer or with a meal.

STEP 13

Today you will meet some of the most attractive and delicious dishes of a vegetarian banquet.

Sabat Gobhi, whole cauliflower surrounded by potato, is enough to make anyone's mouth water while Tahri is an excellent all-in-one rice dish. Gajar Ka Halwa is a very nourishing sweet dish – it is so popular that there is even a book entitled *Dadiji's Carrot Halwa* (Grandmother's Carrot Halwa). It originates from the north of India – North Indians love rich food. Chicken Curry is another dish which is constantly admired by those I have catered for.

❋

SABAT GOBHI

SPICED CAULIFLOWER

SERVES: 4–6

*S*abat Gobhi is a vegetarian party dish (and is equivalent to the whole roasted or tandoori chicken dish). For best results use a firm cauliflower. This dish is medium-hot.

INGREDIENTS:	METRIC	IMPERIAL	AMERICAN
Large garlic cloves	3	3	3
Fresh ginger, chopped	4 cm	$1^{1}/_{2}$ in	$1^{1}/_{2}$ in
Medium onion, chopped	1	1	1

Liquidise the garlic, ginger and onion with 45 ml/3 tbsp water to make a smooth paste.

	METRIC	IMPERIAL	AMERICAN
Medium cauliflower, leaves and stalk cut away	1	1	1
Oil for frying			
Ghee or oil	60 ml	4 tbsp	4 tbsp
Mustard seeds	5 ml	1 tsp	1 tsp
Medium onion, finely chopped	1	1	1
Bay leaves	3	3	3
*Cloves	4	4	4
*Peppercorns	4	4	4
*Cinnamon stick	2.5 ml	1 in	1 in
*Black cardamom	1	1	1
Ground coriander/cilantro	10 ml	2 tsp	2 tsp
Ground roasted cumin	5 ml	1 tsp	1 tsp
Garam masala	5 ml	1 tsp	1 tsp
Ground turmeric	5 ml	1 tsp	1 tsp
Ground red chilli	2.5 ml	$^{1}/_{2}$ tsp	$^{1}/_{2}$ tsp
Ground mace	1.5 ml	$^{1}/_{4}$ tsp	$^{1}/_{4}$ tsp
Ground nutmeg	1.5 ml	$^{1}/_{4}$ tsp	$^{1}/_{4}$ tsp
Salt to taste			
Tomatoes, tinned	400 g	14 oz	14 oz
Potatoes, peeled, washed and cut lengthwise for chips	350 g	12 oz	12 oz

Peas, frozen, or fresh, shelled	225 g	8 oz	2 cups

TO GARNISH:

Green coriander/cilantro leaves, chopped	30 ml	2 tbsp	2 tbsp
Garam masala	5 ml	1 tsp	1 tsp
Small green chilli, chopped	1	1	1

COOKING TIME: 55 MINUTES

1 Heat the ghee or oil in a deep frying pan (skillet) and fry the whole cauliflower on a medium heat until golden brown on all sides. Take it out and keep on one side.

2 Heat the ghee in a large heavy-bottomed pan and add the mustard seeds. When they start crackling, add the chopped onion, bay leaves and the whole spices and fry until golden brown.

3 Mix in the blended paste and fry for a further few minutes until golden brown.

4 Stir in the coriander, cumin, turmeric, garam masala, red chilli, mace, nutmeg and salt and then the tomatoes and fry until all the liquid has been absorbed and the ghee/oil appears on the surface.

5 Put in 50 ml/2 fl oz/3½ tbsp water and cook until all the water is absorbed.

6 Place the cauliflower in the frying pan and cook gently, basting and turning, until tender.

7 Meanwhile, fry the chips in a deep frying pan until golden brown. Boil the peas until tender.

8 Place the cooked cauliflower with sauce in a large serving dish with the chips and the peas.

GARNISH SUGGESTION:

Sprinkle over the garam masala, coriander leaves and the chilli before serving.

SERVING SUGGESTION:

Serve hot with puri, dal, pulao and dahi bara.

TAHRI

UTTAR PRADESH STYLE

SERVES: 2

Tahri is very popular in Uttar Pradish. This rice dish is cooked with a few varieties of vegetables of one's liking. It is a very quick way of preparing a meal in one dish without much hustle and bustle.

INGREDIENTS:	METRIC	IMPERIAL	AMERICAN
Ghee or oil	75 ml	5 tbsp	5 tbsp
Cumin seeds	5 ml	1 tsp	1 tsp
Medium onion, thinly sliced	1	1	1
Vegetables (green/bell pepper, aubergine/eggplant, potato, fresh tomato, cauliflower or any other), cut into 1.2 cm/$\frac{1}{2}$ in pieces	450 g	1 lb	4 cups
Rice (patna or basmati), cleaned, washed and drained	200 g	7 oz	1 cup
Garam masala	10 ml	2 tsp	2 tsp
Ground roasted cumin	5 ml	1 tsp	1 tsp
Ground red chilli	2.5 ml	$\frac{1}{2}$ tsp	$\frac{1}{2}$ tsp
Ground turmeric	2.5 ml	$\frac{1}{2}$ tsp	$\frac{1}{2}$ tsp
Salt to taste			
Water	500 ml	16 fl oz	$2\frac{1}{4}$ cups
Lemon juice	60 ml	4 tbsp	4 tbsp

COOKING TIME: 30 MINUTES

1 Heat the ghee in a heavy-bottomed saucepan on medium heat. Add the cumin seeds and brown them, which will take 2 seconds.

2 Put in the onion and fry until golden brown.

3 Add vegetables and rice and fry for 2 minutes.

4 Mix in the ground spices and salt.

5 Pour in the water. Bring to the boil, reduce the heat to minimum, close the lid and cook for 15 minutes or until tender.

6 Open the lid, tip the pan a little to see if there is any water. If there is, increase the heat to dry it off but do not stir.

7 Remove from heat. Add the lemon juice. Stir gently with a fork. Put the lid back on and serve after 5 minutes.

SERVING SUGGESTION:

Serve hot with pickle or chutney and yoghurt. Paneer tikka and baby aubergines/eggplant go superbly with it.

GAJAR KA HALWA

CARROT HALWA

SERVES: 8

Gajar ka halwa is one of the most attractive, delicious and nourishing sweet dishes from north India.

INGREDIENTS:	METRIC	IMPERIAL	AMERICAN
Carrots, scraped, washed and grated	900 g	2 lb	8 cups
Milk	600 ml	1 pt	$2\frac{1}{2}$ cups
Sugar	200 g	7 oz	1 cup
Ground green cardamom	5 ml	1 tsp	1 tsp
Ghee	60 ml	4 tbsp	4 tbsp
Khoya (page 25)	150 g	5 oz	$\frac{2}{3}$ cup
Almonds, blanched and cut into halves lengthwise	50 g	2 oz	$\frac{1}{3}$ cup
Sultanas/golden raisins	50 g	2 oz	$\frac{1}{3}$ cup
Pistachios, cut into halves lengthwise	25 g	1 oz	2 tbsp

COOKING TIME: 50 MINUTES

1 Place the carrot and the milk in a large heavy-bottomed saucepan on a high heat. Bring to the boil.

2 Reduce the heat to medium and cook, stirring occasionally, until all the milk has been absorbed.

3 Add the sugar (it will make the carrot watery) and green cardamom and cook again until all the liquid is absorbed.

4 Pour in the ghee. Reduce the heat to medium-low and fry for 10 minutes. Stir in the khoya, chopped nuts and sultanas and cook for a further 5 minutes on a low heat.

SERVING SUGGESTION:

Serve hot after a meal.

CHICKEN CURRY

SERVES: 4–6

This recipe is medium-hot and is very tasty and flavoursome. One can taste a lot of Indian herbs. If one wants to eat this with rice, the gravy must be fairly liquid. However, with chapati this should be quite thick.

INGREDIENTS:	METRIC	IMPERIAL	AMERICAN
Oil or ghee	75 ml	5 tbsp	5 tbsp
Medium onions, thinly sliced	2	2	2
Large garlic cloves, chopped	5	5	5
Bay leaves	2	2	2
Fresh ginger, finely chopped	2.5 cm	1 in	1 in
*Cinnamon stick	1.2 cm	$\frac{1}{2}$ in	$\frac{1}{2}$ in
*Cloves	4	4	4
*Peppercorns	4	4	4
*Black cardamom	1	1	1
Chicken, thighs and drumsticks cut into 12 pieces	1 kg	2 lb 4 oz	$4\frac{1}{2}$ cups
Aniseed	15 ml	1 tbsp	1 tbsp
Ground almonds	15 ml	1 tbsp	1 tbsp
Ground coriander/cilantro	15 ml	1 tbsp	1 tbsp
Garam masala	5 ml	1 tsp	1 tsp
Ground cumin	5 ml	1 tsp	1 tsp
Ground red chilli	2.5 ml	$\frac{1}{2}$ tsp	$\frac{1}{2}$ tsp
Ground turmeric	2.5 ml	$\frac{1}{2}$ tsp	$\frac{1}{2}$ tsp
Tomatoes, tinned	400 g	14 oz	$1\frac{3}{4}$ cups
Salt to taste			
Natural yoghurt	150 ml	$\frac{1}{4}$ pt	$\frac{2}{3}$ cup

TO GARNISH:

Garam masala	2.5 ml	$\frac{1}{2}$ tsp	$\frac{1}{2}$ tsp
Green coriander/cilanto leaves, chopped	15 ml	1 tbsp	1 tbsp
Small green chilli, chopped	1	1	1

COOKING TIME: 55 MINUTES

1 Heat the oil or ghee in a large heavy-bottomed saucepan.

2 Add the onions, garlic, bay leaves, ginger, and the whole spices and fry gently until the onion is golden brown on a medium heat.

3 Then add the chicken pieces and fry until they are lightly golden brown on all sides.

4 Stir in the aniseed, ground almonds, coriander, garam masala, roasted cumin, red chilli, turmeric, tomatoes, salt and cook until all the water has been absorbed and the oil/ghee appears on the surface of the mixture.

5 Then add the yoghurt and cook until all the liquid is absorbed.

6 Add 100 ml/3½ fl oz 6½ tbsp water. Cover the pan and simmer on a low heat for about 20 minutes, stirring a few times, until the chicken is tender.

7 Finally add 75 ml/3 fl oz 5 tbsp water. Increase the heat to medium and cook the chicken curry for a further 2 minutes or until required thickness of gravy is obtained. Sprinkle over the garnish before serving.

SERVING SUGGESTION:

Serve hot with chapati or rice, cauliflower, aubergine/eggplant and potato sabji, dahi bara and chutney.

In this step I'll take you to the south of India. Sambar is a nourishing mouthwatering lentil dish prepared with vegetables. In southern India people usually use whole green chillies and make it quite hot but I suggest you make it according to your own taste so that the flavour of the spices can be relished. One can enjoy Sambar with plain rice, but you can add extra flavour to your meal if you prepare Idli. Coconut Chutney is another must with the above dishes. Dried soya mince is a tasty vegetarian alternative to mixed meat, served here with peas. There is also a quick and easy way to serve green/bell pepper and potato.

Rogan Josh is prepared in Kashmiri style. This dish is highly popular with my cookery class. Rogan mirch is a type of chilli which adds more colour to a dish than hotness.

ROGAN JOSH, KASHMIRI STYLE

SERVES: 4–6

This delicious dish is very popular among the Kashmiri community and among the members of my cookery classes. You will find this dish to be medium-hot.

INGREDIENTS:	METRIC	IMPERIAL	AMERICAN
Whole coriander/cilantro	15 ml	1 tbsp	1 tbsp
Cumin seeds	5 ml	1 tsp	1 tsp
Poppy seeds	5 ml	1 tsp	1 tsp
Cloves	4	4	4
Peppercorns	4	4	4
Cinnamon stick	2.5 cm	1 in	1 in
Black cardamom, seeds only	2	2	2

Heat a flat frying pan (skillet) on medium heat and roast the above spices until golden brown. Leave to cool and then grind in a coffee grinder to a powder.

Coconut, desiccated, or fresh, grated	15 ml	1 tbsp	1 tbsp
Ground almonds	15 ml	1 tbsp	1 tbsp
Ground mace	1.5 ml	1/4 tsp	1/4 tsp
Ground nutmeg	1.5 ml	1/4 tsp	1/4 tsp

Heat a flat frying pan (skillet) on medium heat and roast these ingredients until light brown.

Ghee or oil	75 ml	5 tbsp	5 tbsp
Onion seeds (kalonji)	5 ml	1 tsp	1 tsp
Medium onion, finely chopped	1	1	1
Large garlic cloves, crushed	4	4	4
Fresh ginger, finely chopped	2.5 cm	1 in	1 in
Bay leaves	3	3	3
Lamb, boned, cut into 4 cm/1 1/2 in pieces fat trimmed and washed	500 g	1 lb 2 oz	4 1/2 cups

Ground red chilli or rogan mirch	2.5 ml	½ tsp	½ tsp
Ground turmeric	25 ml	½ tsp	½ tsp
Salt to taste			
Tomatoes, tinned	230 g	8 oz	1 cup
Natural yoghurt	150 ml	¼ pt	⅔ cup
Green/bell pepper (cut in 2.5 cm/1 in pieces)	1	1	1
Water	250 ml	8 fl oz	1 cup
Lemon juice	30 ml	2 tbsp	2 tbsp
Sugar	15 ml	1 tbsp	1 tbsp

TO GARNISH:

Garam masala	2.5 ml	½ tsp	½ tsp
Green coriander/cilantro leaves, chopped	15 ml	1 tbsp	1 tbsp
Small green chilli, chopped	1	1	1

COOKING TIME: 40 MINUTES

1 Heat the ghee or oil in a large heavy-bottomed saucepan on medium heat. Fry the onion seeds for 30 seconds. Put in the onion, garlic, ginger and the bay leaves and fry until golden brown. Mix in the meat pieces and fry for 5 minutes.

2 Stir in the red chilli or rogan mirch, turmeric, salt and the roasted ingredients, then the tomatoes and cook until all the liquid has been absorbed and the ghee/oil appears on the surface of the mixture. Add the yoghurt and cook again until all the liquid has reduced.

3 Add the water and green pepper and bring to the boil. Cover and simmer for 10 minutes.

4 Add lemon juice and sugar and cook for 1 minute.

5 Sprinkle over the garnish before serving.

SERVING SUGGESTION:

Serve hot with chapati, rayta, dal, rice and stuffed aubergine/eggplant.

SAMBAR,
SOUTH INDIAN STYLE

SERVES: 4–6

This popular south Indian dish is admired in all parts of India. To make it as hot as the authentic south Indian dish add double the quantity of red chillies.

SAMBAR MASALA:

INGREDIENTS:	METRIC	IMPERIAL	AMERICAN
Coconut, desiccated, or fresh, grated	50 g	2 oz	4 tbsp
Oil	10 ml	2 tsp	2 tsp
Whole coriander/cilantro, cleaned	15 ml	1 tbsp	1 tbsp
Urud ki dhuli dal, cleaned	10 ml	2 tsp	2 tsp
Gram dal (split yellow peas), cleaned	10 ml	2 tsp	2 tsp
Fenugreek seeds	5 ml	1 tsp	1 tsp
Whole small dried red chillies	4	4	4

Heat the oil in a flat frying pan (skillet) on a medium-low heat and roast all the ingredients for 5 minutes or until light brown. Cool it and grind to a fine powder.

SAMBAR:

Arhar dal (tuvar dal), cleaned, washed and drained	250 g	9 oz	$1\frac{1}{2}$ cups
Ground turmeric	5 ml	1 tsp	1 tsp
Salt to taste			
Water	1.2 litres	2 pt	5 cups
Aubergine/eggplant (OR okra), washed, quartered and cut into small pieces	250 g	9 oz	$2\frac{1}{2}$ cups
Tamarind, pulp extracted (see page 24)	75 g	3 oz	3 oz

TARKA:

Oil	90 ml	6 tbsp	6 tbsp
Large pinch of asafoetida			
Mustard seeds	5 ml	1 tsp	1 tsp
Small onions, thinly sliced	3	3	3
Curry leaves OR bay leaves	3	3	3
Garam masala	5 ml	1 tsp	1 tsp
Tomatoes, tinned	400 g	14 oz	1¾ cups
Green coriander/cilantro leaves	90 ml	6 tbsp	6 tbsp

COOKING TIME: 40 MINUTES

1 Place the dal, turmeric, salt and the water into a large saucepan. Bring to the boil, skim off any scum, reduce the heat to medium-low, close the lid and simmer for 30 minutes or until the dal is tender.

2 While the dal is cooking, cook the aubergine or okra in the tamarind pulp, bring to the boil and add the sambar masala.

3 Cook on a medium-low heat for 10 minutes or until the aubergine (or okra) is tender.

4 Mix in the cooked dal.

5 Heat the oil in a saucepan on a medium heat for the tarka (prepare the tarka as well while the dal is cooking). Add the asafoetida and the mustard seeds. When the mustard seeds start crackling, put in the onions and the curry leaves and fry them until lightly brown.

6 Stir in the garam masala and the tomatoes and cook until all the liquid has been absorbed and the oil appears on the surface of the mixture.

7 Add the coriander leaves. Mix in the cooked dal. Bring to the boil, reduce the heat to low and simmer for 5 minutes.

SERVING SUGGESTION:

Serve hot with dosa or idli or rice, rayta and stuffed aubergine/eggplant or cauliflower-potato.

V

GREEN PEPPER AND POTATO

SERVES: 4

This is one of the simplest and the easiest way of cooking green (bell) pepper.

INGREDIENTS:	METRIC	IMPERIAL	AMERICAN
Oil	60 ml	4 tbsp	¼ cup
Small pinch of asafoetida			
Mustard seeds	2.5 ml	½ tsp	½ tsp
Cumin seeds	2.5 ml	½ tsp	½ tsp
Potato, peeled, washed and cut into 2.5 cm/1 in pieces	250 g	9 oz	2¼ cups
Green/bell pepper, washed and cut into 2.5 cm/1 in pieces	250 g	9 oz	2¼ cups
Ground coriander/cilantro	5 ml	1 tsp	1 tsp
Ground roasted cumin	5 ml	1 tsp	1 tsp
Garam masala	2.5 ml	½ tsp	½ tsp
Ground red chilli	2.5 ml	½ tsp	½ tsp
Ground turmeric	1.5 ml	¼ tsp	¼ tsp
Tomatoes, tinned	225 g	8 oz	1 cup
Salt to taste			

TO GARNISH:

Garam masala	1.5 ml	¼ tsp	¼ tsp
Green coriander/cilantro leaves, chopped	15 ml	1 tbsp	1 tbsp
Small green chilli, chopped	1	1	1

COOKING TIME: 20 MINUTES

1 Heat the oil in a large heavy-bottomed saucepan on a medium heat.

2 Add the asafoetida, mustard seeds and the cumin seeds.

3 When the mustard seeds start crackling, add the potato pieces and lightly brown them.

4 Mix in the green pepper and cook for 1 minute.

5 Stir in the ground spices and tomatoes, reduce the heat to low and cook until the vegetables are tender, stirring occasionally.

6 Sprinkle over the garnish before serving.

SERVING SUGGESTION:

Serve hot with dal, rice, puri or chapati and a kofta dish.

SUKHA SOYA KEEMA AUR MATAR

DRIED SOYA MINCE AND PEAS

SERVES: 4

Τhis delicious dish is full of protein and for a vegetarian it is equivalent to minced meat. One can buy dried soya mince from most supermarkets. You will find this dish to be medium-hot.

INGREDIENTS:	METRIC	IMPERIAL	AMERICAN
Oil or ghee	90 ml	6 tbsp	6 tbsp
Medium onions, finely chopped	2	2	2
Large garlic cloves, crushed	3	3	3
Fresh ginger, finely chopped	2.5 cm	1 in	1 in
Dried soya mince, soaked in boiling water 10 minutes before you want to cook, then drained in a sieve	65 g	2.5 oz	1 cup
Peas, frozen, thawed	250 g	10 oz	$2\frac{1}{2}$ cups
Garam masala	5 ml	1 tsp	1 tsp
Ground coriander/cilantro	10 ml	2 tsp	2 tsp
Ground roasted cumin	5 ml	1 tsp	1 tsp
Ground red chilli	2.5 ml	$\frac{1}{2}$ tsp	$\frac{1}{2}$ tsp
Ground turmeric	2.5 ml	$\frac{1}{2}$ tsp	$\frac{1}{2}$ tsp
Salt to taste			
Tomatoes, tinned, chopped	400 g	14 oz	$1\frac{3}{4}$ cups

TO GARNISH:

Green coriander/cilantro leaves, chopped	30 ml	2 tbsp	2 tbsp
Garam masala	2.5 ml	$\frac{1}{2}$ ml	$\frac{1}{2}$ ml
Green chilli, chopped	1	1	1

COOKING TIME: 30 MINUTES

1 Heat the oil or ghee in a heavy-bottomed saucepan on medium heat. Add the onions, garlic and ginger and fry until golden brown.

2 Put in the drained soya mince and peas and fry for 1 minute.

3 Stir in spices and tomatoes and cook until all the liquid has been absorbed and the oil/ghee appears on the top of the mixture.

4 Sprinkle over the garnish.

SERVING SUGGESTION:

Serve hot with naan, rayta, pulao and green lentils.

IDLI

SOUTH INDIAN BREAD

MAKES: 12

This plain rice and lentil bread cooked in steam is the speciality of south India. It goes superbly with hot sambar and coconut chutney. A south Indian meal is not complete without idli. If you do not have idli containers, use egg poaching cups and stand them on a trivet.

INGREDIENTS:	METRIC	IMPERIAL	AMERICAN
Rice, cleaned, washed and soaked overnight	150 g	5 oz	1 cup
Urud ki dhuli dal, cleaned, washed and soaked	75 g	3 oz	½ cup
Water	225 ml	8 fl oz	1 cup

Combine the above ingredients in a blender and blend them to make a thick smooth paste.

Large pinch of salt

Add the salt to the lentil and rice paste and whip this for 5 minutes. Cover and keep in a warm place for 24 hours.

COOKING TIME: 35 MINUTES

1 Boil some water (water level should be under idli containers) in a large saucepan.

2 Grease idli containers with a little oil.

3 Pour 30 ml/2 tbsp idli mixture into each container.

4 Close the lid and steam cook for 30 minutes or until tender.

SERVING SUGGESTION:

Serve hot with sambar, coconut chutney and mixed vegetable korma.

STEP 15

D hansak is popular dish which can be enjoyed by both vegetarians and non-vegetarians, depending on the version cooked. After cooking, one can either purée the lentils and vegetables or leave them as they are.

My recipe for Fried Bhindi is quick and easy. Because it is a dry dish, it is highly suitable for any type of packed lunch or picnic. Another advantage of its dry nature is that it does not go off quickly. Bhuni Seviya is a sweet dish which is very simple and easy to make. Likewise Sabudana Papa are easy to make. These can be stored.

✳ DHANSAK

SERVES: 4–6

This delightful dish is cooked with different varieties of lentils and vegetables. Dhansak is not only delicious but also rich in food minerals.

INGREDIENTS:	METRIC	IMPERIAL	AMERICAN
Chicken, boned, skinned, cut into 5 cm/2 in pieces and washed	800 g	1³/₄ lb	2¹/₃ cups
Dals (use five or six types of different lentils e.g. moong (split yellow peas), gram, masoor (red lentils), tuvar, green whole moong and black whole urud), about 25 g/ 1 oz/2 tbsp each), cleaned, soaked overnight and washed	150 g	6 oz	³/₄ cup
Ground turmeric	2.5 ml	¹/₂ tsp	¹/₂ tsp
Salt to taste			
Vegetables (use four different e.g. green/bell pepper, aubergine/ eggplant, mushroom and marrow/squash), peeled, washed and cut into large pieces	200 g	7 oz	1³/₄ cups
Methi (green fenugreek leaves)	45 ml	3 tbsp	3 tbsp
Mint leaves	45 ml	3 tbsp	3 tbsp
Coriander/cilantro leaves	45 ml	3 tbsp	3 tbsp
Coconut, desiccated, or fresh, grated	30 ml	2 tbsp	2 tbsp
Medium onions, finely chopped	2	2	2
Large garlic cloves, crushed	5	5	5
Fresh ginger, finely chopped	2.5 cm	1 in	1 in
Water	900 ml	1¹/₂ pts	3²/₃ cups
Ghee or oil	90 ml	6 tbsp	6 tbsp
Mustard seeds	5 ml	1 tsp	1 tsp
Cumin seeds	5 ml	1 tsp	1 tsp

Garam masala	10 ml	2 tsp	2 tsp
Ground coriander/cilantro	10 ml	2 tsp	2 tsp
Ground roasted cumin	5 ml	1 tsp	1 tsp
Ground red chilli	5 ml	1 tsp	1 tsp
Ground sambar masala	15 ml	1 tbsp	1 tsp
Ground turmeric	2.5 ml	$\frac{1}{2}$ tsp	$\frac{1}{2}$ tbsp
Salt to taste			
Tomatoes, tinned	400 g	14 oz	$1\frac{3}{4}$ cups
Lemon juice	60 ml	4 tbsp	4 tbsp
Water	150 ml	$\frac{1}{4}$ pt	$\frac{2}{3}$ cup

TO GARNISH:

Garam masala	2.5 ml	$\frac{1}{2}$ tsp	$\frac{1}{2}$ tsp
Small green chilli, chopped	1	1	1

COOKING TIME: 1 HOUR 10 MINUTES

1 Place the chicken, dals, turmeric, salt, vegetables, methi, mint, coriander, coconut, half the onions, the garlic and ginger with the water on a medium heat. Bring to the boil, skim off any scum, reduce the heat to medium-low, close the lid and cook for 40 minutes or until the chicken is tender.

2 Take out the chicken pieces and cook the lentil mixture for a further 20 minutes or until the lentils are tender.

3 Leave it to cool, then either use as it is or put in a blender to make a smooth paste.

4 While the lentil mixture is cooking, heat the ghee or oil in a saucepan on a medium heat. Add the mustard seeds and, when they start crackling, brown the cumin seeds. Put in the rest of the onion and gently fry until golden brown.

5 Mix in the cooked chicken pieces and fry for 5 minutes or until light brown.

6 Stir in the garam masala, coriander, roasted cumin, red chilli, sambar masala, turmeric, salt and tomatoes and cook for a further 2 minutes.

7 Pour in the ground lentil paste, lemon juice and water. Bring to the boil, reduce the heat to medium-low and cook for a further 10 minutes or until the required consistency is obtained.

8 Sprinkle over the garnish before serving.

SERVING SUGGESTION:

Serve hot with rice, puri, pumpkin kofta and rayta.

✳ VEGETARIAN DHANSAK

SERVES 4–6

This version replaces the meat with paneer, but it is equally delicious and nutritious.

INGREDIENTS:	METRIC	IMPERIAL	AMERICAN
Dals (use five or six types of different lentils e.g. moong (split yellow peas), gram, masoor (red lentils), tuvar, green whole moong and black whole urud), about 25g/1 oz/2 tbsp each, cleaned, soaked overnight and washed	150 g	6 oz	1 cup
Ground turmeric	2.5 ml	½ tsp	½ tsp
Salt to taste			
Vegetables (use four different e.g. green/bell pepper, aubergine/eggplant, mushroom and marrow/squash), peeled, washed and cut into large pieces	200 g	7 oz	1¾ cups
Methi (green fenugreek leaves)	45 ml	3 tbsp	3 tbsp
Mint leaves	45 ml	3 tbsp	3 tbsp
Coriander/cilantro leaves	45 ml	3 tbsp	3 tbsp
Coconut, desiccated, or fresh, grated	30 ml	2 tbsp	2 tbsp
Medium onions, finely chopped	2	2	2
Large garlic cloves, crushed	3	3	3
Fresh ginger, finely chopped	2.5 cm	1 in	1 in
Water	900 ml	1½ pts	3⅔ cups
Ghee or oil	90 ml	6 tbsp	6 tbsp
Mustard seeds	5 ml	1 tsp	1 tsp
Cumin seeds	5 ml	1 tsp	1 tsp

Paneer (see page 23) cut into 1.2 cm/½ in cubes	225 g	8 oz	1 cup
Garam masala	10 ml	2 tsp	2 tsp
Ground coriander/cilantro	10 ml	2 tsp	2 tsp
Ground roasted cumin	5 ml	1 tsp	1 tsp
Ground red chilli	5 ml	1 tsp	1 tsp
Ground sambar masala	15 ml	1 tbsp	1 tbsp
Ground turmeric	2.5 ml	½ tsp	½ tsp
Salt to taste			
Tomatoes, tinned	400 g	14 oz	1¾ cups
Lemon juice	60 ml	4 tbsp	4 tbsp

TO GARNISH:

Garam masala	2.5 ml	½ tsp	½ tsp
Small green chilli, chopped	2.5 ml	½ tsp	½ tsp

COOKING TIME: 1 HOUR 10 MINUTES

1 Place the dals, turmeric, salt, vegetables, methi, mint, coriander, coconut, half the onions, the garlic and ginger with the water on a medium heat. Bring to the boil, skim off any scum, reduce the heat to medium-low, close the lid and cook for 1 hour or until the dal is tender.

2 Leave it to cool and then put in a blender to make a smooth paste.

3 While the lentil mixture is cooking, heat the ghee or oil in a saucepan on a medium heat. Add the mustard seeds and when they start crackling, brown the cumin seeds. Put in the rest of the onion and gently fry until golden brown.

4 Mix in the paneer pieces and fry for 2 minutes or until light brown.

5 Stir in the garam masala, coriander, roasted cumin, red chilli, sambar masala, turmeric, salt and tomatoes and cook for a further 2 minutes.

STEP
15

6 Pour in the ground lentil paste and lemon juice. Bring to the boil, reduce the heat to medium-low and cook for a further 10 minutes or until the required consistency is obtained. Sprinkle over the garnish before serving.

SERVING SUGGESTION:

Serve hot with rice, puri, pumpkin kofta and rayta.

V

FRIED BHINDI

NORTH INDIAN-STYLE LADIES' FINGER

SERVES: 4

*C*ooked in this way okra is delicious and crispy, so don't be put off by the sticky nature of the fresh vegetable.

INGREDIENTS:	METRIC	IMPERIAL	AMERICAN
Oil	75 ml	5 tbsp	5 tbsp
Medium onions, finely chopped	3	3	3
Fresh ginger, finely chopped	2.5 cm	1 in	1 in
Tender okra/ladies' fingers, washed, dried, the ends trimmed and cut into 1 cm/$\frac{1}{2}$ in round pieces	500 g	18 oz	$4\frac{1}{2}$ cups
Ground coriander/cilantro	13 ml	1 tbsp	1 tbsp
Ground roasted cumin	5 ml	1 tsp	1 tsp
Ground turmeric	2.5 ml	$\frac{1}{2}$ tsp	$\frac{1}{2}$ tsp
Ground red chilli	2.5 ml	$\frac{1}{2}$ tsp	$\frac{1}{2}$ tsp
Garam masala	2.5 ml	$\frac{1}{2}$ tsp	$\frac{1}{2}$ tsp
Salt to taste			

TO GARNISH:

Garam masala	2.5 ml	$\frac{1}{2}$ tsp	$\frac{1}{2}$ tsp
Small green chilli	1	1	1

COOKING TIME: 20 MINUTES

1 Heat the oil in a frying pan (skillet) on medium heat and lightly brown the onions and the ginger.

2 Add the okra pieces and fry for a further 5 minutes.

3 Add the coriander, cumin, turmeric, red chilli, garam masala and salt. Cook on low heat for a further 5–7 minutes or until tender. Keep turning.

4 Sprinkle over the garnish before serving.

SERVING SUGGESTION:

Serve hot with paratha or puri, dal, rayta, rice and a meat dish.

✳ SABUDANA PAPAR

TAPIOCA PAPADUM

MAKES: 22

Sabudana Papar are quite easy to make and they complement all sorts of meals. I have made them very mild but one can add coarsely ground peppercorns and ground red chilli (according to taste) to make them hot.

INGREDIENTS:	METRIC	IMPERIAL	AMERICAN
Tapioca	50 g	2 oz	$^1/_3$ cup
Salt	1.5 ml	$^1/_4$ tsp	$^1/_4$ tsp
Water	500 ml	17 fl oz	$2^1/_4$ cups
Food colour, yellow, red, green or blue (optional)			
Oil for frying			

COOKING TIME: 10 MINUTES

1 Place the tapioca, water and the salt (and food colour if using) in a saucepan on medium heat. Stir continuously until all the water has been absorbed. One can check this in two ways. While stirring, the mixture will leave the edge of the pan. Alternatively, if you drop a little cooked tapioca from a spoon it joins together and falls in a lump.

2 Turn off the heat. Take 15 ml/1 tbsp of cooked tapioca and place it on a greased tray. It should spread itself thinly to form a circle about 7.5 cm/ 3 in in diameter. If it doesn't, it means that you have over-cooked it. Don't worry: add an extra 100 ml/3 fl oz/6 tbsp water and boil it again.

3 Place 11 papars on each tray. Leave them to dry.

4 On the next day they will be loose on the tray. Turn them over. After drying, the tapioca papars shrink in size.

STEP
15

5 Heat the oil in a deep frying pan (skillet) on medium-high heat. When the oil is very hot, gently slip a dried papar in the hot oil and it will increase 3 times in size. Fry it very light brown on both sides (it will take a few seconds only). Fry them before serving and they will be crispy and crunchy. Do not fry too far in advance because papars tend to go soft very quickly. When completely dried, keep them in an airtight container.

SERVING SUGGESTION:

Serve hot or at room temperature with a meal or at tea time.

BHUNI SEVIYA

ROASTED VERMICELLI

SERVES: 4

When I was three years old my grandmother taught me how to take a tiny piece of dough, twist it into a fine thread and leave it in the sun to dry. When the vermicelli was cooked I used to climb on to my father's lap and pick out the strands I made from his pudding!

INGREDIENTS:	METRIC	IMPERIAL	AMERICAN
Milk	500 ml	16 fl oz	2$\frac{1}{4}$ cups
Sugar	50 g	2 oz	$\frac{1}{4}$ cup
Ground green cardamom	2.5 ml	$\frac{1}{2}$ tsp	$\frac{1}{2}$ tsp
Roasted vermicelli, broken	60 g	$\frac{1}{2}$ oz	$\frac{1}{4}$ cup

COOKING TIME: 10 MINUTES

1 Place the milk, sugar and green cardamom in a saucepan to boil on medium heat.

2 When the milk starts boiling add broken strands of vermicelli and cook for a further 3 minutes.

SERVING SUGGESTION:

Serve hot after a meal.

T his step introduces some items of the chāt family. Chāt is popular all over India. It is sold on the roadside, served in restaurants and even in smart hotels. Chāt can be eaten at any time by anyone – on plates and on leaves, with a fork or with the hand. As children in Britain spend their money on chocolate, in the same way children in India, spend their money on chāt. One can always see a long queue in front of the chāt stalls. Chāt is spicy, crunchy, and sweet and sour in taste.

❋
ALOO KI TIKIYA

NORTH INDIAN-STYLE POTATO PATTIES

MAKES: 12

Tikiya is an appetising item for tea and for chāt especially during winter and the rainy seasons. They are very easy to make and one can buy them from hawkers in the streets and railway stations of India. You will find this dish to be medium-hot.

PREPARING THE POTATO COATING:

INGREDIENTS:	METRIC	IMPERIAL	AMERICAN
Potatoes, boiled in jackets, peeled and mashed	500 g	1 lb 2 oz	2¼ cups
Green coriander/cilantro leaves, chopped	15 ml	1 tbsp	1 tbsp
Garam masala	2.5 ml	½ tsp	½ tsp
Ground red chilli	2.5 ml	½ tsp	½ tsp
Ground roasted cumin	2.5 ml	½ tsp	½ tsp
Small green chilli, chopped (optional)	1	1	1
Salt to taste			

Place the above ingredients in a bowl. Mix them together thoroughly and divide into 12 equal portions.

PREPARING THE PEAS FILLING:

Oil	30 ml	2 tbsp	2 tbsp
Mustard seeds	2.5 ml	½ tsp	½ tsp
Cumin seeds	5 ml	1 tsp	1 tsp
Ground red chilli	1.5 ml	¼ tsp	¼ tsp
Ground coriander/cilantro	5 ml	1 tsp	1 tsp
Ground roasted cumin	5 ml	1 tsp	1 tsp
Salt to taste			
Peas, fresh, shelled, or frozen	250 g	9 oz	2¼ cups
Lemon juice	30 ml	2 tbsp	2 tbsp

Garam masala	5 ml	1 tsp	1 tsp
Green chilli chopped	1	1	1
Green coriander/cilantro leaves, chopped	15 ml	1 tbsp	1 tbsp

1 Heat the oil in a heavy-bottomed saucepan. Add the mustard seeds and when they start crackling, brown the cumin seeds.

2 Stir in the red chilli, ground cumin, ground coriander, salt and the peas.

3 When the peas are cooked stir in the lemon juice, garam masala, green chilli and the coriander leaves. Divide into 12 equal portions.

PREPARING THE TIKIYAS:

Oil for frying

FRYING TIME: 35 MINUTES

1 Take 1 portion of the mashed potato and roll it into a ball in the palms of your hands, flatten the ball and place a portion of the peas filling into the centre. Bring the edges over and smoothly cover the filling. Make into a ball again and flatten until it is a 1.2 cm/½ in thick circle. Repeat and finish the mixture.

2 Heat a flat frying pan (skillet) on a medium heat and smear with 30 ml/2 tbsp oil. Place 5 or 6 tikiyas on it.

3 When the underneath is golden brown, turn them over carefully.

4 Pour 15–30 ml/1–2 tbsp more oil all around the tikiyas and fry the other side as well until golden brown.

SERVING SUGGESTION:

Serve hot with chutney, gulab jamun, balushahi and dalmod at tea.

GOL GUPPA

MAKES: 24

Gol Guppa are one of the delicious items of the 'chāt'. It is difficult to find a single street in India where a hawker is not selling chāt. In the main shopping areas, one finds several hawkers sitting next to each other (as close as 2 metres apart) selling this popular snack.

PREPARING THE FILLING:

INGREDIENTS:	METRIC	IMPERIAL	AMERICAN
Chickpeas/garbanzos, boiled	75 g	2 oz	½ cup
Potatoes, boiled in jackets, peeled and cut into tiny pieces	75 g	3 oz	½ cup
Green coriander/cilantro leaves, chopped	15 ml	1 tbsp	1 tbsp
Salt to taste			

Place the above ingredients into a bowl. Mix them thoroughly and set the bowl on one side.

PREPARING THE GOL GUPPA:

Brown chapati flour (wheat flour)	50 g	2 oz	½ cup
Semolina/cream of wheat	25 g	1 oz	¼ cup
Lemon juice	2.5 ml	½ tsp	½ tsp
Small pinch of salt			
Water, lukewarm	50 ml	2 fl oz	¼ cup
Oil for frying			

1 Place the above ingredients in a bowl. Mix thoroughly. Knead the dough with the warm water for 3–5 minutes or until the dough is springy and satiny. Cover and leave for 30 minutes.

2 Shape the dough into a ball and then roll into a thin circle on an oiled board.

3 Cut several circles of 6 cm/2½ in in diameter. Repeat until you have used all the dough.

4 Take a tea towel and soak it in water. Spread it on an upturned tray. Spread the small circles on the tea towel and cover with another wet tea towel and leave for 5 minutes.

COOKING TIME: 30 MINUTES

1 Heat the oil in a deep frying pan (skillet) on medium heat. Put one circle into the hot oil, sinking it gently under the oil using a slotted spoon. As soon as it comes up like a balloon, put another one in.

2 Fry 4 or 5 together until golden brown and crispy. Keep turning them over.

3 Leave them to cool on a cooling tray. The gol guppas can be kept for two weeks in an airtight tin.

PREPARING THE GOL GUPPA KA PANI (SPICY WATER OF THE GOL GUPPA):

Green coriander/cilantro leaves	15 ml	1 tbsp	1 tbsp
Fresh mint	15 ml	1 tbsp	1 tbsp
Water	300 ml	1/2 pt	1 1/4 cups
Sugar	10 ml	2 tsp	2 tsp
Garam masala	2.5 ml	1/2 tsp	1/2 tsp
Ground red chilli	2.5 ml	1/2 tsp	1/2 tsp
Ground roasted cumin	2.5 ml	1/2 tsp	1/2 tsp
Tamarind pulp, thick (see page 24)	15 ml	1 tbsp	1 tbsp
Lemon juice	15 ml	1 tbsp	1 tbsp
Salt to taste			

1 Combine the coriander and mint leaves in a blender and blend with 60 ml/4 tbsp water until you have a smooth paste.

2 Pour the rest of the water into a jug and add all the above ingredients. Mix it thoroughly.

3 Dilute to your taste and keep in a refrigerator for 2–3 hours before using.

SERVING SUGGESTION:

Make a small hole in each gol guppa and fill it with the filling mixture. Dip it in the pani and eat at once.

PAPRI

MAKES: 24

The papri can be eaten as a snack or as one of the items of chāt. It is very crispy and delicious. In India young girls spend most of their pocket money on chāt and then on a chocolate or a sweet. In every school and college, one will find at least one chāt stall with a long queue of keen buyers during lunch time and later in front of the chāt hawkers outside the school. Papri will keep for two weeks in an airtight container.

INGREDIENTS:	METRIC	IMPERIAL	AMERICAN
Plain/all-purpose flour, sifted	250 g	8 oz	2 cups
Lemon juice	5 ml	1 tbsp	1 tbsp
Tymol seeds (ajwain)	5 ml	1 tbsp	1 tbsp
Water, lukewarm	120 ml	4 fl oz	½ cup
Salt	1.5 ml	¼ tsp	¼ tsp

Place 200 g/7 oz/1¼ cups of the flour and the rest of the ingredients in a bowl. Knead the dough with water for 5 minutes or until the dough is soft, springy and satiny. Cover and leave it for 30 minutes.

Oil for frying

COOKING TIME: 40 MINUTES

1 Divide the dough into 24 equal portions. Take a portion and roll it into a ball in the palms of your hands, flatten it, put a few drops of oil on the rolling board and roll it into a thin circle.

2 Smear the top with 2.5 ml/½ tsp oil, sprinkle with dry flour and fold in half (giving a half moon shape).

3 Smear the top again with oil and sprinkle on the dry flour and fold again. Then roll the whole thing out thinly in a triangle shape about 5 mm/¼ in thick.

4 Heat the oil in a deep frying pan (skillet) on a medium-low heat. Slip 4–5 papris gently into the hot oil from the edge of the pan.

5 Keep turning them over and fry until light brown and crispy. Roll the papris for the next batch while one batch is frying.

SERVING SUGGESTION:

Serve it as it is at tea or serve it as a 'chat'. Place 15ml/1 tbsp of gol guppa filling on the papri. Pour 15 ml/1 tbsp whisked natural yoghurt and 5 ml/1 tsp tamarind chutney over it. Sprinkle garam masala, red chilli, ground roasted cumin over and eat at once otherwise it will become soggy.

FRUIT CHĀT

SERVES: 4–6

*F*ruit chāt is very nourishing and appetising. We used to make it every afternoon after the meal especially in the guava season. It is nice to make fruit chāt with several varieties of fruit but one can make it with as few as two different fruits. You will find this fruit chāt to be medium-hot.

INGREDIENTS:	METRIC	IMPERIAL	AMERICAN
Apples, washed and cut into 2.5 cm/1 in pieces	100 g	4 oz	1 cup
Pears, washed and cut into 2.5 cm/1 in pieces	100 g	4 oz	1 cup
Guavas washed and cut into 2.5 cm/1 in pieces	100 g	4 oz	1 cup
Grapes (preferably seedless)	100 g	4 oz	1 cup
Bananas	3	3	3
Lemon juice	30 ml	2 tbsp	2 tbsp
Sugar	15 ml	1 tbsp	1 tbsp
Large pinch of garam masala			
Large pinch of ground red chilli			
Salt to taste			

PREPARATION TIME: 10 MINUTES

Place all the above ingredients in a bowl. Mix well and serve it cold. Other fruits which can be used for chāt are pineapple, orange, papaya, apricot, peach and melon.

SERVING SUGGESTION:

Serve after a meal. It is an exciting way of eating fresh fruits.

T his step combines a selection of
vegetarian and non-vegetarian dishes.
Malai Murgi is a chicken dish with cream,
nuts and spices which is just superb. Chola Dal
cooked in this East Indian style gives it a flavour
unique to itself. Bharta cooked in this North Indian
style is also irresistible. Perhaps you can make a
night of it and cook the aubergine in the hot ashes
of a bonfire.
Gujrati-style Dokri completes the menu.

MALAI MURGI

CREAMED CHICKEN WITH NUTS

SERVES: 6

*T*his creamed chicken dish is a treasure from the Indian cuisine. It is an oriental delight for you and your guests. You will find this dish to be medium-hot.

INGREDIENTS:	METRIC	IMPERIAL	AMERICAN
Ghee or oil	75 ml	5 tbsp	5 tbsp
Large garlic cloves, crushed	4	4	4
Fresh ginger, finely chopped	4 cm	1$\frac{1}{2}$ in	1$\frac{1}{2}$ in
Medium onions, finely chopped	3	3	3
Bay leaves	3	3	3
Cloves	4	4	4
*Cinnamon stick	2.5 cm	1 in	1 in
*Black cardamom	1	1	1
*Peppercorns	4	4	4
Chicken, skinned, washed and cut into 16 pieces	1.4 kg	3 lb	3 lb
Garam masala	5 ml	1 tsp	1 tsp
Ground roasted cumin	5 ml	1 tsp	1 tsp
Ground red chilli	2.5 ml	$\frac{1}{2}$ tsp	$\frac{1}{2}$ tsp
Ground turmeric	2.5 ml	$\frac{1}{2}$ tsp	$\frac{1}{2}$ tsp
Ground nutmeg	1.5 ml	$\frac{1}{4}$ tsp	$\frac{1}{4}$ tsp
Ground mace	1.5 ml	$\frac{1}{4}$ tsp	$\frac{1}{4}$ tsp
Salt to taste			
Milk	300 ml	$\frac{1}{2}$ pt	1$\frac{1}{4}$ cups
Almonds, blanched and cut in halves lengthwise	75 g	3 oz	$\frac{3}{4}$ cup
Cashew-nuts, cut in halves lengthwise	75 g	3 oz	$\frac{3}{4}$ cup
Pistachios, cut in halves lengthwise	25 g	1 oz	2 tbsp
Raisins	150 g	5 oz	$\frac{3}{4}$ cup
Ground green cardamom	2.5 ml	$\frac{1}{2}$ tsp	$\frac{1}{2}$ tsp

Cream (single/light)	300 ml	10 fl oz	1¼ cups

TO GARNISH:

Garam masala	2.5 ml	½ tsp	½ tsp
Green coriander/cilantro leaves, finely chopped	15 ml	1 tbsp	1 tbsp
Small green chilli, finely chopped	1	1	1

COOKING TIME: 40 MINUTES

1 Heat the ghee or oil in a large heavy-bottomed saucepan. Put in the garlic, ginger, onions, bay leaves, cloves, cinnamon, black cardamom and peppercorns and fry gently until golden brown.

2 Add the chicken pieces and fry for about 10 minutes until lightly golden brown on all sides.

3 Stir in garam masala, roasted cumin, red chilli, turmeric, nutmeg, mace, salt and milk.

4 Bring it to the boil. Reduce the heat to medium-low and cover the pan. Cook for 15 minutes, stirring occasionally.

5 Open the lid and add the chopped almonds, cashew-nuts, and pistachios, raisins and the cardamom and fry on medium heat until all the liquid has been absorbed and the ghee/oil appears on the top of the mixture and the chicken is tender.

6 Reduce the heat to low and pour in the cream. Allow to simmer for 2 minutes.

7 Sprinkle over the garnish.

SERVING SUGGESTION:

Serve hot with rice, puri, stuffed aubergine/eggplant and salad.

CHOLA DAL

SPLIT YELLOW PEAS
BENGALI STYLE

SERVES: 4–6

*C*hola Dal (gram dal or split yellow peas) is very popular among all Indians although the way of cooking is slightly different in various parts of India. I think that the Bengali style of this cooked lentil is absolutely delicious. It gives a unique sweet and sour taste.

INGREDIENTS:	METRIC	IMPERIAL	AMERICAN
Gram dal, cleaned, washed and soaked for an hour	250 g	9 oz	1½ cups
Ground turmeric	2.5 ml	½ tsp	½ tsp
Water	1.7 litres	3 pts	7½ cups
Salt to taste			

TARKA:

Oil	45 ml	3 tbsp	3 tbsp
Cumin seeds	5 ml	1 tsp	1 tsp
Small onion, finely chopped	1	1	1
Fresh ginger, finely chopped	1.2 cm	½ in	½ in
Bay leaves	2	2	2
Coconut, desiccated, or fresh, grated	50 g	2 oz	½ cup
Garam masala	2.5 ml	½ tsp	½ tsp
Ground red chilli	2.5 ml	½ tsp	½ tsp
Ground turmeric	1.5 ml	¼ tsp	¼ tsp
Small green chilli, finely chopped	1	1	1
Sugar	25 g	1 oz	¼ cup
Tamarind, pulp (see page 24)	25 g	1 oz	2 tbsp

TO GARNISH:

Green coriander/cilantro leaves	15 ml	1 tbsp	1 tbsp
Garam masala	2.5 ml	½ tsp	½ tsp

COOKING TIME: 1 HOUR

1 Put the dal in a large saucepan with the turmeric, water and the salt. Bring to the boil, skim off any scum and simmer on a medium heat for 50 minutes or until tender.

2 While the dal is cooking prepare the tarka. Heat the oil in a heavy-bottomed saucepan, add the cumin seeds and brown them.

3 Add the onion, ginger and bay leaves and fry until light brown.

4 Stir in the coconut and fry it until golden brown.

5 Add the garam masala, red chilli, turmeric, green chilli, sugar and the tamarind pulp.

6 Bring the mixture to the boil and add it to the cooked lentils.

7 Stir and simmer for a further 10 minutes. The texture of the lentils should not be too thick. Sprinkle over the garnish before serving.

SERVING SUGGESTION:

Serve hot with plain rice, okra, rayta and a meat or fish dish.

BHARTA

MASHED AUBERGINE, NORTH INDIAN STYLE

SERVES: 4–6

*F*or Bharta one needs large aubergines/eggplants. In this recipe one needs to bake the aubergines in the oven. In India, most Indians still use wood or coal for cooking, therefore normally people roast an aubergine under hot ashes – roasting this way adds extra taste to the dish. You will find this dish to be medium-hot.

INGREDIENTS:	METRIC	IMPERIAL	AMERICAN
Oil	60 ml	4 tbsp	4 tbsp
Mustard seeds	2.5 ml	$^1/_2$ tsp	$^1/_2$ tsp
Cumin seeds	2.5 ml	$^1/_2$ tsp	$^1/_2$ tsp
Large garlic cloves, crushed	3	3	3
Medium onions, finely chopped	2	2	2
Fresh ginger, finely chopped	2.5 cm	1 in	1 in
Large aubergine/eggplant, baked or roasted at 200°C/400°F/gas mark 6, peeled and mashed	500 g	18 oz	$4^1/_2$ cups
Ground coriander/cilantro	30 ml	2 tbsp	2 tbsp
Ground red chilli	2.5 ml	$^1/_2$ tsp	$^1/_2$ tsp
Ground turmeric	1.25 ml	$^1/_4$ tsp	$^1/_2$ tsp
Garam masala	2.5 ml	$^1/_2$ tsp	$^1/_2$ tsp
Salt to taste			
Tomatoes, tinned	400 g	14 oz	$1^3/_4$ cups
Peas, frozen, or fresh, shelled	250 g	9 oz	$2^1/_4$ cups

TO GARNISH:

	METRIC	IMPERIAL	AMERICAN
Garam masala	2.5 ml	$^1/_2$ tsp	$^1/_2$ tsp
Green coriander/cilantro leaves, chopped	15 ml	1 tbsp	1 tbsp
Small green chilli, chopped	1	1	1

COOKING TIME: 30 MINUTES

1 Heat the oil in a heavy-bottomed saucepan.

2 Add the mustard seeds and fry them until they crackle.

3 Add the cumin seeds, then the garlic, onions and the ginger and fry gently on a medium heat until they are lightly brown.

4 Stir in the mashed aubergine and cook for a further 2 minutes.

5 Then add the coriander, red chilli, turmeric, garam masala, salt and the tomatoes and cook until all the water has been absorbed and the oil appears on the top of the mixture.

6 Stir in the peas and simmer for 5 minutes or until the peas are tender.

7 Sprinkle over the garnish before serving.

SERVING SUGGESTION:

Serve hot with puri or chapati, rice, dal and a chicken dish.

V

✳ DOKRI

GUJRATI STYLE

SERVES 4–6

Dokri is a speciality of Gujrat but it is enjoyed in the other parts of India. Indian cooks often use Eno, the liver salts you can buy from chemists.

INGREDIENTS:	METRIC	IMPERIAL	AMERICAN
Gram flour, sifted	100 g	4 oz	1 cup
Natural yoghurt	150 ml	1/4 pt	2/3 cup
Garam masala	2.5 ml	1/2 tsp	1/2 tsp
Ground ginger	2.5 ml	1/2 tsp	1/2 tsp
Ground red chilli	2.5 ml	1/2 tsp	1/2 tsp
Ground turmeric	2.5 ml	1/2 tsp	1/2 tsp
Small green chilli, chopped (optional)	1	1	1
Salt to taste			

Place the sifted flour in a bowl. Gradually add the yogurt to make a smooth batter. Mix in the spices. Cover and keep overnight.

Eno	2.5 ml	1/2 tsp	1/2 tsp
Water	1.2 litres	2 pts	5 cups

TARKA:

Oil	30 ml	2 tbsp	2 tbsp
Large pinch of asafoetida			
Mustard seeds	2.5 ml	1/2 tsp	1/2 tsp
Cumin seeds	2.5 ml	1/2 tsp	1/2 tsp
Sesame seeds	2.5 ml	1/2 tsp	1/2 tsp
Sugar	5 ml	1 tsp	1 tsp
Citric acid	2.5 ml	1/2 tsp	1/2 tsp

COOKING TIME: 20 MINUTES

1 Place the water and a trivet in a large saucepan. Make sure that the water level is below the trivet.

2 Bring to the boil on a medium heat.

3 Add the Eno to the batter, whip well, then place the batter in a heatproof container about 1.2 cm/ ½ in high.

4 Place the container on the trivet.

5 Close the lid and cook for 15 minutes or until cooked. (Check with a fork or knife. Push it in the dokri. If it hasn't got any sticky flour on it when you take it out it is cooked). It should rise to double its size and be soft and spongy.

6 Take a sharp knife and cut into 2.5 cm/1 in pieces. Turn the dish over and remove all the pieces without breaking.

PREPARING THE TARKA:

1 While the dokri is cooking, prepare the tarka.

2 Heat the oil in a saucepan.

3 Add the asafoetida and the mustard seeds and when the mustard seeds start crackling brown the cumin seeds and the sesame seeds.

4 Add the cooked dokri pieces. Mix it thoroughly. Turn the heat off.

5 Mix in the sugar and the citric acid.

SERVING SUGGESTION:

Serve hot or cold at tea with chutney, gulab jamun and barfi.

STEP
18

Nearing the end of your 21 steps, I shall now allow you to try a real vegetarian delight: Bharwa Shimla Ki Meerch, green/bell pepper stuffed with potatoes and raisins, cooked in a sweet and sour sauce. Aloo Katchori is another of those dishes suitable for all occasions and the picnic basket.

It is quick and easy to make. Keema Gobhi is a tasty cauliflower side dish. Keema Kebab is a meat dish and can be eaten as a starter or as a dish with a meal.

BHARWA SHIMLA KI MEERCH

STUFFED GREEN PEPPER

SERVES: 4–6

*T*he stuffed green/bell pepper is one of my delicious party
dishes. It looks very attractive on the dinner table.
it takes a long time to prepare, therefore I do two or
three things together, like boiling the potatoes when I
am cooking something else and preparing the sauce while
the stuffed peppers are cooking. The potatoes and the
sauce can be prepared the day before. This dish is
medium-hot.

INGREDIENTS:	METRIC	IMPERIAL	AMERICAN
Small green/bell peppers, washed.	500 g	1 lb 2 oz	18 oz

Cut a small cap from the stem end of each paper.
Scoop out the seeds.

PREPARING THE FILLING:

Oil	75 ml	5 tbsp	5 tbsp
Mustard seeds	5 ml	1 tsp	1 tsp
Cumin seeds	5 ml	1 tsp	1 tsp
Potatoes, boiled in jackets, peeled and cut into small pieces	1 kg	2 lb 4 oz	4½ cups
Ground coriander/cilantro	30 ml	2 tbsp	2 tbsp
Ground roasted cumin	5 ml	1 tsp	1 tsp
Ground red chilli	2.5 ml	½ tsp	½ tsp
Ground turmeric	2.5 ml	½ tsp	½ tsp
Salt to taste			
Garam masala	5 ml	1 tsp	1 tsp
Raisins	100 g	4 oz	½ cup
Lemon juice	30 ml	2 tbsp	2 tbsp
Sugar	10 ml	2 tsp	2 tsp

Green coriander/cilantro leaves, chopped	15 ml	1 tbsp	1 tbsp
Small green chilli, chopped	1	1	1

COOKING TIME: 10 MINUTES

1 Heat the oil in a frying pan (skillet). Add the mustard seeds. When they start to crackle add the cumin seeds and the potato pieces and fry them on medium heat for 2–3 minutes.

2 Stir in the coriander, roasted cumin, red chilli, turmeric, salt and garam masala and fry for a further 2–3 minutes.

3 Add the raisins, lemon juice, sugar, coriander leaves and green chilli and cook for 1 minute. Turn the heat off and set the pan on one side.

PREPARING THE SAUCE:

Large onion, coarsely chopped	1	1	1
Large garlic cloves, coarsely chopped	3	3	3
Fresh ginger, coarsely chopped	1.2 cm	½ in	½ in

Combine the large onion, garlic cloves and fresh ginger pieces in a blender with 60 ml/4 tbsp water and blend to make a fine paste.

Oil	60 ml	4 tbsp	4 tbsp
Mustard seeds	2.5 ml	½ tsp	½ tsp
Small onion, finely chopped	1	1	1
Ground coriander/cilantro	10 ml	2 tsp	2 tsp
Garam masala	5 ml	1 tsp	1 tsp
Ground red chilli	2.5 ml	½ tsp	½ tsp
Ground turmeric	2.5 ml	½ tsp	½ tsp
Salt to taste			
Tomatoes, tinned	400 g	14 oz	1¾ cups
Tamarind, thick pulp (see page 24)	30 ml	2 tbsp	2 tbsp
Sugar	15 ml	1 tbsp	1 tbsp

TO GARNISH:

Garam masala	2.5 ml	½ tsp	½ tsp
Green coriander/cilantro leaves	15 ml	1 tbsp	1 tbsp
Small green chilli	1	1	1

COOKING TIME: 35 MINUTES

1 Heat the oil in a large frying pan (skillet) and add the mustard seeds.

2 When the seeds start to crackle, add the chopped onion and fry on medium heat until golden brown.

3 Stir in the blended paste and fry again until golden brown.

4 Then add the coriander, garam masala, red chilli, turmeric, salt and the tomatoes and cook until the oil appears on the top of the mixture.

5 Stuff the peppers with the potato filling, place the tops back on. Place the stuffed peppers in the sauce, put the lid on the pan and cook on medium-low heat for 15 minutes, until the peppers are cooked. While cooking, baste with sauce and turn over 3 or 4 times.

6 Stir in the tamarind pulp and sugar and cook until all the liquid has been absorbed.

TO GARNISH:

Place the stuffed peppers in a circle in a 5 cm/2 in deep serving dish, leaving some gaps between each pepper. Place the leftover potato mixture and sauce in each gap. Sprinkle over the garnish.

SERVING SUGGESTION:

Serve hot with lentils, rice, puri or onion paratha and a chicken dish.

✳

KEEMA KEBAB

MAKES: 10

This is one of the delicious lamb minced meat dishes which can be served as a side dish with a meal, or at tea-time. In this dish, mince is first cooked with lentils and spices and then blended to a very fine paste. The size of the kebab depends on individual choice. You will find this dish to be medium-hot.

PREPARING THE MEAT PASTE:

INGREDIENTS:	METRIC	IMPERIAL	AMERICAN
Keema (minced lamb)	250 g	9 oz	$^3/_4$ cup
Gram dal (split yellow peas), soaked overnight in 500 ml/ 17 fl oz/2$^1/_4$ cups water	75 g	3 oz	$^1/_2$ cup
Medium onion, coarsely chopped	1	1	1
Large garlic clove, coarsely chopped	1	1	1
Fresh ginger, coarsely chopped	2.5 cm	1 in	1 in
Garam masala	10 ml	2 tsp	2 tsp
Ground red chilli	2.5 ml	$^1/_2$ tsp	$^1/_2$ tsp
Salt to taste			

1 Place all the above ingredients with 350 ml/ 12 fl oz/1½ cups water in a saucepan on a medium heat. Bring to the boil. Reduce the heat to medium-low and cook for 30 minutes or until the dal and meat are tender (if more water is needed, bring it to the boil first before adding).

2 Dry off any remaining liquid over a high heat.

3 When cold, place a little at a time in a blender and blend to make a smooth paste.

4 Divide into 10 equal portions.

PREPARING THE FILLING:

Medium onion, finely chopped	1	1	1
Small green chilli, finely chopped	1	1	1
Green coriander/cilantro leaves, chopped	45 ml	3 tbsp	3 tbsp

Place the above ingredients on a plate and mix them thoroughly. Divide the mixture into 10 equal portions.

Oil for frying	

FRYING TIME: 25 MINUTES

1 Place a few drops of oil on the palm of your hand.

2 Take a portion of meat paste, flatten it, place 1 portion of filling on it, bring the edges over to cover, roll tightly in a ball and flatten to 5 mm/¼ in thick. Make all the kebabs in the same manner.

3 Heat a flat frying pan (skillet) on a medium heat. Smear with 15 ml/1 tbsp oil, reduce the heat to medium-low and put in 4–6 kebabs.

4 Turn them over gently after 2 minutes. Pour in 15 ml/1 tbsp oil around the kebabs and fry the other side as well until golden brown. I don't turn the kebabs over more than 2–3 times.

SERVING SUGGESTION:

Serve hot with a meal or at tea with chutney.

✳ ALOO KATCHORI

DEEP-FRIED POTATO BREAD

MAKES: 20

Aloo Katchori is an interesting variation of puri. It is a hearty bread and very popular in Uttar Pradesh. You will find this bread to be medium-hot.

PREPARING THE DOUGH:

INGREDIENTS:	METRIC	IMPERIAL	AMERICAN
Chapati flour, brown	250 g	9 oz	$2^1/_4$ cups
Margarine	25 g	1 oz	2 tbsp
Natural yoghurt	30 ml	2 tbsp	2 tbsp
Tymol seeds (ajwain), cleaned	2.5 ml	$^1/_2$ tsp	$^1/_2$ tsp
Large pinch of salt			
Water, lukewarm	100 ml	$3^1/_2$ fl oz	$6^1/_2$ tbsp

Place the flour into a bowl. Add the margarine and mix thoroughly. Put in the rest of the ingredients and pour in the water to make a soft dough. Knead it for 5 minutes or until the dough is springy and satiny. Cover and leave for 30 minutes.

PREPARING THE FILLING:

	METRIC	IMPERIAL	AMERICAN
Potatoes, boiled in jackets, peeled and mashed	500 g	1 lb 2 oz	$4^1/_2$ cups
Ground roasted cumin	5 ml	1 tsp	1 tsp
Garam masala	2.5 ml	$^1/_2$ tsp	$^1/_2$ tsp
Tymol seeds (ajwain), cleaned	2.5 ml	$^1/_2$ tsp	$^1/_2$ tsp
Ground red chilli	1.5 ml	$^1/_4$ tsp	$^1/_4$ tsp
Salt to taste			
Green coriander/cilantro leaves, chopped	30 ml	2 tbsp	2 tbsp
Small green chilli, finely chopped	1	1	1

STEP
18

Place the mashed potato, ground spices, salt and the chopped ingredients in a bowl and mix them thoroughly.

Oil for frying

COOKING TIME: 35 MINUTES

1 Heat the oil in a deep frying pan (skillet) on medium heat. While the oil is heating, divide the dough into 20 equal portions.

2 Take a portion of dough, roll it into a ball with the palms of your hands and flatten it. Put a few drops of oil on the rolling board and roll into 5 cm/2 in diameter circle.

3 Place 1 portion of filling on the dough and cover the filling by bringing the edges together.

4 Again flatten, put a few drops of oil on the rolling board and roll it into a round 5 mm/¼ in thick (with a rolling pin or by patting with your fingers).

5 Slip the aloo katchori gently into the hot oil from the edge of the pan. Gently press the aloo katchori with a slotted spoon all over and it will swell up a little.

6 Fry both sides light brown.

SERVING SUGGESTIONS:

Serve hot at a meal with a vegetable dish, dahi bara, chutney and pickle. The aloo katchoris are ideal to be taken on a picnic.

KEEMA GOBHI

GRATED CAULIFLOWER

SERVES: 4–6

Keema Gobhi is an interesting and delicious way of cooking a cauliflower. Whenever I want to increase the quantity, I add peas, which go very well with cauliflower.

INGREDIENTS:	METRIC	IMPERIAL	AMERICAN
Oil or ghee	75 ml	5 tbsp	5 tbsp
Mustard seeds	5 ml	1 tsp	1 tsp
Onion seeds (kalonji)	5 ml	1 tsp	1 tsp
Medium onion, finely chopped	1	1	1
Large garlic cloves, crushed	2	2	2
Fresh ginger, finely chopped	2.5 cm	1 in	1 in
Medium cauliflower, washed and finely grated	1	1	1
Ground coriander/cilantro	10 ml	2 tsp	2 tsp
Ground roasted cumin	5 ml	1 tsp	1 tsp
Ground red chilli	2.5 ml	$\frac{1}{2}$ tsp	$\frac{1}{2}$ tsp
Ground turmeric	2.5 ml	$\frac{1}{2}$ tsp	$\frac{1}{2}$ tsp
Garam masala	2.5 ml	$\frac{1}{2}$ tsp	$\frac{1}{2}$ tsp
Ground mace	1.5 ml	$\frac{1}{4}$ tsp	$\frac{1}{4}$ tsp
Ground nutmeg	1.5 ml	$\frac{1}{4}$ tsp	$\frac{1}{4}$ tsp
Salt to taste			

TO GARNISH:

Garam masala	2. 5 ml	$\frac{1}{2}$ tsp	$\frac{1}{2}$ tsp
Green coriander/cilantro leaves, chopped	15 ml	1 tbsp	1 tbsp
Small green chilli, chopped	1	1	1

COOKING TIME: 30 MINUTES

1 Heat the oil in a large frying pan (skillet) on a medium heat.

2 Add the mustard seeds and when they start crackling brown the onion seeds which will take about 2 seconds.

3 Put in the onion, garlic and ginger, and fry them until lightly brown.

4 Mix in the cauliflower and cook for 5 minutes. Stir in the ground spices and salt and mix thoroughly.

5 Close the lid, reduce the heat to low and steam-cook for 20 minutes or until tender, stirring occasionally.

6 Sprinkle over the garnish before serving.

SERVING SUGGESTION:

Serve hot with chapati or puri, dhaniya-pudeena ka rayta and a kofta dish.

STEP 19

Now I will teach you to prepare Chicken Tikka without a tandoori oven. If you like to eat this with sauce see the Murgh Musallum recipe. For vegetarians there is Gajar-Matar Ki Sabji, a nourishing and delicious carrot and peas dish, and Khadi which is spicy sour yoghurt. In this step you will learn to prepare Gujiya, another very popular sweet. This is often prepared during festivals in India.

CHICKEN TIKKA

*C*hicken tikka is one of the most popular dishes of my cookery class. One can eat it as a starter or as a side dish with a meal. You will find this dish to be quite hot.

INGREDIENTS:	METRIC	IMPERIAL	AMERICAN
Large garlic cloves	4	4	4
Fresh ginger	2.5 cm	1 in	1 in
Lemon juice	15 ml	1 tbsp	1 tbsp
Natural yoghurt	150 ml	1/4 pt	2/3 cup
Ground turmeric	2.5 ml	1/2 tsp	1/2 tsp
Ground red chilli	5 ml	1 tsp	1 tsp
Ground coriander/cilantro	15 ml	1 tbsp	1 tbsp
Ground roasted cumin	15 ml	1 tbsp	1 tbsp
Garam masala	5 ml	1 tsp	1 tsp
Salt to taste			
Sugar	15 ml	1 tbsp	1 tbsp
Chicken breast (skinned, boned, washed and cut into 10 cm/4 in pieces)	450 g	1 lb	1 lb
Ghee for basting			

1 Grind the garlic and ginger with the lemon juice and yoghurt to make a fine paste.

2 Add the turmeric, red chilli, coriander, cumin, garam masala, salt and sugar to the paste and mix well.

3 Rub the ground paste into the chicken pieces and marinate them for 6–8 hours.

4 Roast the chicken pieces in the oven (200°C/ 400°F/gas mark 6), for half an hour or until cooked, basting every so often with ghee and turning them every 10 minutes.

5 If you want to eat with sauce see the stuffed Murgh Musallum recipe (page 72).

GAJAR-
MATAR KI SABJI

CARROT AND PEAS, NORTH INDIAN STYLE

SERVES: 4

This nourishing vegetable dish is cooked in every part of India but by different methods in different areas. In the west of India onion and garlic are avoided but lemon and sugar are added instead. You will find this dish to be medium-hot.

INGREDIENTS:	METRIC	IMPERIAL	AMERICAN
Oil	60 ml	4 tbsp	4 tbsp
Mustard seeds	5 ml	1 tsp	1 tsp
Cumin seeds	5 ml	1 tsp	1 tsp
Large garlic cloves, crushed	2	2	2
Fresh ginger, finely chopped	1.2 cm	$\frac{1}{2}$ in	$\frac{1}{2}$ in
Medium onion, finely chopped	1	1	1
Ground coriander/cilantro	10 ml	2 tsp	2 tsp
Garam masala	5 ml	1 tsp	1 tsp
Ground red chilli	2.5 ml	$\frac{1}{2}$ tsp	$\frac{1}{2}$ tsp
Ground turmeric	2.5 ml	$\frac{1}{2}$ tsp	$\frac{1}{2}$ tsp
Salt to taste			
Tomatoes, tinned	400 g	14 oz	$1\frac{3}{4}$ cups
Tender small carrots, washed and cut into 2.5 cm/1 in pieces	500 g	1 lb	$4\frac{1}{2}$ cups
Peas, frozen, or fresh, shelled	250 g	9 oz	$2\frac{1}{4}$ cups

TO GARNISH:

Garam masala	2.5 ml	$\frac{1}{2}$ tsp	$\frac{1}{2}$ tsp
Green coriander/cilantro leaves, chopped	15 ml	1 tbsp	1 tbsp
Small green chilli, chopped	1	1	1

COOKING TIME: 30 MINUTES

1 Heat the oil in a large heavy-bottomed saucepan.

2 Add the mustard seeds and when they start crackling brown the cumin seeds.

3 Put in the garlic, ginger and onion and fry gently on medium heat until golden brown.

4 Stir in the coriander, garam masala, red chilli, turmeric and salt and then the tomatoes and the carrots.

5 Close the lid, reduce the heat to medium-low and cook for 10 minutes or until the carrot pieces are slightly tender, stirring occasionally.

6 Mix in the peas and cook for a further few minutes until the peas are tender and the oil appears on the surface of the mixture.

7 Increase the heat and dry off any remaining water.

8 Sprinkle over the garnish before serving.

SERVING SUGGESTION:

Serve hot with dal, rice, puri, rayta and a fish dish.

KHADI

NORTH INDIAN-PUNJABI STYLE

SERVES: 4–6

This delightful dish is a mixture of gram flour and sour yoghurt. It is very refreshing and appetising. In western India 15 ml/1 tbsp sugar is added to kadhi.

INGREDIENTS:	METRIC	IMPERIAL	AMERICAN
Gram flour, sifted	25 g	1 oz	2 tbsp
Garam masala	2.5 ml	$^{1}/_{2}$ tsp	$^{1}/_{2}$ tsp
Ground ginger	2.5 ml	$^{1}/_{2}$ tsp	$^{1}/_{2}$ tsp
Ground red chilli	2.5 ml	$^{1}/_{2}$ tsp	$^{1}/_{2}$ tsp
Ground turmeric	2.5 ml	$^{1}/_{2}$ tsp	$^{1}/_{2}$ tsp
Salt to taste			
Natural yoghurt, kept for 2 or 3 days so that it becomes sour	450 ml	$^{3}/_{4}$ pt	2 cups

Place the sifted gram flour and the spices in a bowl and gradually blend in the yoghurt.

PAKORA MIXTURE:

Gram flour, sifted	150 g	5 oz	$1^{1}/_{4}$ cups
Garam masala	5 ml	1 tsp	1 tsp
Ground red chilli	2.5 ml	$^{1}/_{2}$ tsp	$^{1}/_{2}$ tsp
Tymol seeds (ajwain) cleaned	2.5 ml	$^{1}/_{2}$ tsp	$^{1}/_{2}$ tsp
Salt to taste			
Small onions, thinly sliced	2	2	2
Water	100 ml	$3^{1}/_{2}$ fl oz	$6^{1}/_{2}$ tbsp
Oil	15 ml	1 tbsp	1 tbsp
Oil for frying			

Place the flour, spices and onions in a bowl. Gradually pour in the water to make smooth batter. Stir in the oil. Heat the oil in a deep frying pan (skillet) on a medium-high heat.

STEP
19

Slip 15 ml/1 tbsp batter in the hot oil and fry 7 or 8 pakoras together until golden brown. Take them out with a slotted spoon, place them on a cooling tray and set them on one side.

Oil	60 ml	4 tbsp	4 tbsp
Large pinch of asafoetida			
Cumin seeds	5 ml	1 tsp	1 tsp
Water	1 litre	1¾ pts	4½ cups

TARKA:

Ghee	90 ml	6 tbsp	6 tbsp
Mustard seeds	2.5 ml	½ tsp	½ tsp
Small onion, finely chopped	1	1	1
Garam masala	5 ml	1 tsp	1 tsp
Green coriander/cilantro leaves, chopped	45 ml	3 tbsp	3 tbsp
Small green chilli, chopped	1	1	1

COOKING TIME: 40 MINUTES

1 Heat the oil in a large heavy-bottomed saucepan on a medium heat. Add the asafoetida and when it starts sizzling brown the cumin seeds.

2 Pour in the gram flour and yoghurt mixture with half the water.

3 Keep on stirring until it starts boiling.

4 Add the fried pakoras and the remaining water.

5 Bring to the boil, reduce the heat to medium-low and cook for a further 25 minutes or until the required consistency has been obtained. Indians like to eat kadhi as runny as soup with plain rice.

6 While the kadhi is cooking, prepare the tarka. Heat the ghee in a saucepan on a medium heat.

7 Add the mustard seeds and when they start crackling fry the onion until golden brown.

8 Turn the heat off and stir in the garam masala, coriander leaves and the green chilli. Pour the tarka on the kadhi before serving.

SERVING SUGGESTION:

Serve hot with plain rice, pickle or chutney, okra and stuffed aubergine/eggplant.

STEP
19

PLAIN RICE

SERVES 4–6

Manju (my younger sister) won't have her meal without plain rice and dal, and therefore it is cooked daily in my parents' house. Sajni likes it very much and when she was little used to call it white rice, and the name has stuck! It is very easy to make.

INGREDIENTS:	METRIC	IMPERIAL	AMERICAN
Rice (patna or basmati), cleaned, washed and drained	200 g	7 oz	scant 1 cup
Water	375 ml	13½ fl oz	1½ cups
Ghee	15 ml	1 tbsp	1 tbsp

COOKING TIME: 20 MINUTES

1 Place the rice, water and ghee in a saucepan. Bring it to the boil on a medium heat.

2 Reduce the heat to low, cover the pan and cook for 15 minutes. If any water is left, dry it off on a high heat but don't stir.

3 Turn the heat off and leave for 5 minutes at least before serving.

SERVING SUGGESTION:

Turn over the cooked rice gently with a fork (to separate the grains). Serve hot with dal, or kadhi, vegetable curries, yoghurt and pickle.

GUJIYA

MAKES: 16

This is an elegant sweet snack which is specially prepared by most Hindus to celebrate the auspicious festival of Diwali (the festival of lights and fireworks) and Holi (the festival of colour).

PREPARING THE DOUGH:

INGREDIENTS:	METRIC	IMPERIAL	AMERICAN
Margarine	25 g	1 oz	2 tbsp
Plain/all-purpose flour	100 g	4 oz	1 cup
Water, lukewarm	60 ml	2½ fl oz	¼ cup

Rub the margarine into the flour. Pour in the water and knead for 2 minutes or until the dough is soft, springy and satiny. Cover and leave for 30 minutes.

PREPARING THE FILLING:

Ghee	7.5 g	1½ tsp	1½ tsp
Sultanas/golden raisins	50 g	2 oz	⅓ cup
Almonds, blanched and finely chopped	25 g	1 oz	¼ cup
Pistachios, finely chopped	15 g	½ oz	2 tbsp
Khoya (see page 25) made from full cream milk powder	75 g	3 oz	⅓ cup
Sugar	75 g	3 oz	⅓ cup
Ground green cardamom	2.5 ml	½ tsp	½ tsp
Saffron (soaked in 15 ml/ 1 tbsp warm milk)	1.5 ml	¼ tsp	¼ tsp

1 Heat the ghee in a saucepan on medium-low heat and fry the sultanas and chopped nuts for 2 minutes.

2 Mix in the khoya, sugar, cardamom and the saffron and cook for a further 3 minutes, stirring continuously. Turn the heat off. Set the pan on one side to cool.

PREPARING THE GUJIYA:

Ghee and oil for frying (equal quantities)

COOKING TIME: 1 HOUR

1 Heat the fat in a deep frying pan (skillet) on medium-low heat. While the fat is heating, divide the dough and the filling into 16 equal portions.

2 Take a portion of dough and roll into a ball on the palms of your hands, flatten it and thinly roll it about 11.5 cm/4½ in round in diameter (do not use flour or oil for rolling).

3 Place 1 portion of filling on a round of dough.

4 Lift 1 side gently and fold over (giving a half moon shape), press both the edges to seal and pinch with your fingers to give an attractive pattern.

5 Slip the gujiya gently into the hot fat from the edge of the pan. Make another gujiya and add to the fat, then turn them over only 3 or 4 times.

6 Fry 4 or 5 gujiya together until lightly golden brown on all sides. Keep on making them but cook immediately, do not keep them on the rolling board after making but cook immediately. Leave them to cool on a cooling tray.

SERVING SUGGESTION:

Serve hot or cold after a meal or at tea with dalmod and pakora.

This step offers Machli Ki Sabji, a perfect choice for fish-lovers. English fish flakes very easily, so I have adapted the recipe slightly. Fish dishes are very popular in Bengal and usually people eat fish daily. Red beans are cooked in Punjab very regularly, more so than in any other part of India. Puri Walé Aloo is very simple to prepare and this curry is absolutely delicious. Vegetarians can enjoy Sukhe Masalé Dar Paneer, a dry and spicy paneer dish.

Machli Ki Sabji

FISH CURRY

SERVES: 4–6

This fish dish is very delicious and easy to make. The spices add flavour to the bland fish. Take care when frying the fish pieces. Turn them over two or three times only.

PREPARING THE FISH PIECES:

INGREDIENTS:	METRIC	IMPERIAL	AMERICAN
Large garlic cloves, chopped	4	4	4
Medium onions, cut into large pieces	2	2	2
Fresh ginger, chopped	2.5 cm	1 in	1 in
Vinegar	50 ml	2 fl oz	3$\frac{1}{2}$ tbsp
Fish (cod or haddock), boned, cut into 4 cm/1$\frac{1}{2}$ in pieces and washed	500 g	1 lb 2 oz	4$\frac{1}{2}$ cups
Oil for frying			

Combine the garlic, onions, ginger in a blender and blend to make a fine paste. Divide the paste into 2 portions. Marinate the fish pieces in one of the ground paste portions for 1 hour. Set the other portion to one side for the sauce.

FRYING TIME: 30 MINUTES

1 Heat 45 ml/3 tbsp oil in a flat frying pan (skillet). Place in half of the marinated fish pieces and fry on a medium heat for 15 minutes or until light brown.

2 Turn them over 2 or 3 times only. Take them out with a slotted spoon and place them on the serving dish. Do the same with the rest of the fish.

PREPARING THE SAUCE:

Oil	60 ml	4 tbsp	4 tbsp
Mustard seeds	5 ml	1 tsp	1 tsp
Small onion, finely chopped	1	1	1
Bay leaves	2	2	2
*Cloves	4	4	4
*Peppercorns	4	4	4
*Black cardamom	1	1	1
*Cinnamon stick	1.2 cm	1 in	1 in
Garam masala	5 ml	1 tsp	1 tsp
Ground coriander/cilantro	5 ml	1 tsp	1 tsp
Ground roasted cumin	5 ml	1 tsp	1 tsp
Ground turmeric	5 ml	1 tsp	1 tsp
Ground red chilli	2.5 ml	½ tsp	½ tsp
Salt to taste			
Tomatoes, tinned	230 g	8 oz	1 cup
Natural yoghurt	150 ml	¼ pt	⅔ cup
Water	120 ml	4 fl oz	½ cup
Lemon	15 ml	1 tbsp	1 tbsp
Sugar	15 ml	1 tbsp	1 tbsp

TO GARNISH:

Garam masala	2.5 ml	½ tsp	½ tsp
Green coriander/cilantro leaves, chopped	15 ml	1 tbsp	1 tbsp
Small green chilli, finely chopped	1	1	1

COOKING TIME: 30 MINUTES

1 Prepare the sauce while the fish is marinating. Heat the oil in a large heavy-bottomed saucepan on medium heat. Add the mustard seeds and when they start crackling fry the chopped onion, bay leaves, cloves, peppercorns, black cardamom and cinnamon stick until golden brown.

2 Mix in the blended paste and fry for a further few minutes until golden brown.

3 Stir in the garam masala, coriander, roasted cumin, turmeric, red chilli, salt and the tomatoes and cook until all the liquid has been absorbed.

4 Put in the yoghurt and cook again until all the liquid is absorbed and the oil appears on the surface of the mixture.

5 Pour in the water, bring it to the boil, then add lemon and sugar and cook for a further 2 minutes. Pour the sauce over the fried fish pieces and sprinkle over the garnish before serving.

SERVING SUGGESTION:

Serve hot with chapati, rice, dal, rayta and a bean-potato dish.

PURI
WALÉ ALOO

POTATO CURRY

SERVES: 4

This is a most simple and delicious dish. You will find this dish to be medium-hot.

INGREDIENTS:	METRIC	IMPERIAL	AMERICAN
Oil or ghee	60 ml	4 tbsp	4 tbsp
Mustard seeds	2.5 ml	$\frac{1}{2}$ tsp	$\frac{1}{2}$ tsp
Cumin seeds	2.5 ml	$\frac{1}{2}$ tsp	$\frac{1}{2}$ tsp
Potatoes, boiled in jackets, peeled and cut into 5 mm/ $\frac{1}{4}$ in pieces	500 g	1 lb 2 oz	$4\frac{1}{2}$ cups
Ground coriander/cilantro	5 ml	1 tsp	1 tsp
Ground roasted cumin	5 ml	1 tsp	1 tsp
Garam masala	2.5 ml	$\frac{1}{2}$ tsp	$\frac{1}{2}$ tsp
Ground red chilli	2.5 ml	$\frac{1}{2}$ tsp	$\frac{1}{2}$ tsp
Ground turmeric	2.5 ml	$\frac{1}{2}$ tsp	$\frac{1}{2}$ tsp
Salt to taste			
Tomatoes, tinned	400 g	14 fl oz	$1\frac{3}{4}$ cups
Water	150 ml	$\frac{1}{4}$ pt	$\frac{2}{3}$ cup
Lemon juice	15 ml	1 tbsp	1 tbsp

TO GARNISH:

Garam masala	2.5 ml	$\frac{1}{2}$ tsp	$\frac{1}{2}$ tsp
Green coriander/cilantro leaves, chopped	15 ml	1 tbsp	1 tbsp
Small green chilli, chopped	1	1	1

COOKING TIME: 20 MINUTES

1 Heat the oil or ghee in a heavy-bottomed saucepan. Add the mustard seeds and when they start crackling add the cumin seeds and fry for a few seconds until they are golden brown.

2 Mix in the potato pieces and fry them until light brown.

3 Stir in the ground coriander, roasted cumin, garam masala, red chilli, turmeric, salt and tomatoes and cook until all the liquid has been absorbed.

4 Pour in the water and bring to boil. Reduce the heat to low and simmer it for 2 minutes.

5 Add the lemon juice.

6 Sprinkle over the garnish before serving.

SERVING SUGGESTION:

Serve hot with puri, jalebi, lassi and pickle at breakfast or at any meal.

RAJMA

RED BEANS, NORTH INDIAN STYLE

SERVES: 4–6

Red beans, rajma, and black-eyed beans are some of the best and richest sources of protein especially for vegetarians. They are very tasty and most Punjabis cook them at least once a week. Sometimes I add a handful of whole black urud lentils as well before soaking. This dish is medium-hot.

INGREDIENTS:	METRIC	IMPERIAL	AMERICAN
Large garlic cloves, chopped	3	3	3
Fresh ginger, chopped	2.5 cm	1 in	1 in
Medium onion, coarsely chopped	1	1	1

Combine the garlic, ginger and onion in a blender with 45 ml/3 tbsp water and blend to make a smooth paste.

	METRIC	IMPERIAL	AMERICAN
Rajma, cleaned and soaked overnight	250 g	9 oz	1½ cups
Salt to taste			
Water	2.75 litres	5 pts	12 cups
Ghee or oil	90 ml	6 tbsp	6 tbsp
Small onion, finely chopped	1	1	1
Bay leaves	2	2	2
*Cloves	4	4	4
*Peppercorns	4	4	4
*Cinnamon stick	1.2 cm	1 in	1 in
*Black cardamom	1	1	1
Garam masala	2.5 ml	½ tsp	½ tsp
Ground coriander/cilantro	5 ml	1 tsp	1 tsp
Ground roasted cumin	5 ml	1 tsp	1 tsp
Ground red chilli	2.5 ml	½ tsp	½ tsp
Ground turmeric	2.5 ml	½ tsp	½ tsp
Salt to taste			
Tomatoes, tinned	150 g	5 oz	⅔ cup

TO GARNISH:

Garam masala	2.5 ml	½ tsp	½ tsp
Green coriander/cilantro leaves, chopped	15 ml	1 tbsp	1 tbsp
Small green chilli, chopped	1	1	1

COOKING TIME: 1 HOUR 35 MINUTES

1 Place the soaked rajma, salt and the water in a large saucepan (if the pan is not large enough then add boiling water as needed) on medium heat. Bring to the boil, reduce the heat to medium-low, close the lid and cook for 1 hour 20 minutes or until the rajma are tender.

2 Prepare the sauce while the rajma are cooking.

3 Heat the ghee or oil in a large heavy-bottomed saucepan on a medium heat. Fry the finely chopped onion, bay leaves, cloves, peppercorns, cinnamon and cardamom and until golden brown.

4 Put in the blended paste and fry for a further few minutes until golden brown.

5 Stir in garam masala, coriander, roasted cumin, red chilli, turmeric, salt and then the tomatoes and cook until all the liquid has been absorbed and the ghee/oil appears on the surface of the mixture.

6 Add the cooked rajma and cook for a further 15 minutes or until the required thickness of sauce is obtained.

7 Sprinkle over the garnish before serving.

SERVING SUGGESTION:

Serve hot with plain rice, chapati, cauliflower, rayta and a chicken dish.

❋ SUKHE MASALÉ DAR PANEER

DRY SPICY PANEER

SERVES: 4

This delicious paneer dish is very popular in my family. It is rich in food value and taste. You will find this dish medium-hot.

INGREDIENTS:	METRIC	IMPERIAL	AMERICAN
Paneer (see page 23)	3.4 litres	6 pts	15 cups

Cut the paneer into 2.5 cm/1 in long and 5 mm/¼ in thick pieces and bake at them in a hot oven 200°C/400°F/gas mark 6 for 10 minutes

Oil 90 ml	6 tbsp	6 tbsp	
Cumin seeds	5 ml	1 tsp	1 tsp
Medium onions, finely chopped	2	2	2
Large garlic cloves, crushed	4	4	4
Fresh ginger, chopped	2.5 cm	1 in	1 in
Ground coriander/cilantro	10 ml	2 tsp	2 tsp
Garam masala	5 ml	1 tsp	1 tsp
Ground roasted cumin	5 ml	1 tsp	1 tsp
Ground red chilli	2.5 ml	½ tsp	½ tsp
Ground turmeric	2.5 ml	½ tsp	½ tsp
Salt to taste			
Tomatoes, tinned, mashed	400 g	14 oz	1¾ cups

TO GARNISH:

Green chilli, finely chopped	1	1	1
Green coriander/cilanto, finely chopped	30 ml	2 tbsp	2 tbsp
Garam masala	2.5 ml	1 tsp	1 tsp

COOKING TIME: 15 MINUTES

1 Heat the oil in a heavy-bottomed saucepan on medium heat. Add the cumin seeds to brown (which will take 2 seconds).

2 Add the onions, garlic and ginger and fry until golden brown.

3 Stir in the ground spices, salt, tomatoes and paneer pieces and cook until all the liquid has been absorbed and oil appears on the surface of the mixture.

4 Sprinkle over the garnish.

SERVING SUGGESTION:

Serve hot with any type of bread, lentils, rice dish and onion, cucumber and tomato rayta.

To complete your 21 steps to Indian cookery I shall introduce you to a new and original meat dish Sukha Masalé Wala Gosht. Dry meat masala is very popular amongst all meat lovers. For vegetarians Bharwa Tomatar, stuffed tomatoes is just the thing for you. Vegetable Biriyani and a vegetarian keema can also be prepared today. The flavours of the above dishes give great credit to the cook if they are cooked well.

I'll end a hard day's work with just one more dish – Rasgulla. Many Asians find this dish difficult to prepare, but if you follow the recipe carefully you will achieve good results. Good luck and happy cooking!

SUKHA MASALÉ WALA GOSHT

DRY MEAT MASALA

SERVES: 4–6

This is a popular dish from the northern cuisine of India. In dry meat masala, the meat is cooked separately and then matured in spices and onion. It is full of flavour. You will find this dish quite hot.

INGREDIENTS:	METRIC	IMPERIAL	AMERICAN
Meat (lamb shoulder, boneless), cut into 2.5 cm/1 in pieces, trimmed of fat and washed	500 g	1 lb 2 oz	4½ cups
Ghee or oil	75 ml	5 tbsp	5 tbsp
Onion seeds	5 ml	1 tsp	1 tsp
Sesame seeds	5 ml	1 tsp	1 tsp
Bay leaves	4	4	4
Large garlic cloves, crushed	3	3	3
Fresh ginger, finely chopped	2.5 cm	1 in	1 in
Medium onions, finely chopped	2	2	2
Ground almonds	15 ml	1 tbsp	1 tbsp
Ground coriander/cilantro	15 ml	1 tbsp	1 tbsp
Ground roasted cumin	5 ml	1 tsp	1 tsp
Garam masala	5 ml	1 tsp	1 tsp
Ground red chilli	2.5 ml	½ tsp	½ tsp
Ground turmeric	2.5 ml	½ tsp	½ tsp
Ground mace	1.5 ml	¼ tsp	¼ tsp
Ground nutmeg	1.5 ml	¼ tsp	¼ tsp
Salt to taste			

TO GARNISH:

Garam masala	2.5 ml	½ tsp	½ tsp
Green coriander/cilantro leaves, chopped	15 ml	1 tbsp	1 tbsp
Small green chilli, chopped	1	1	1

COOKING TIME: 45 MINUTES

1 Place the meat pieces with 400 ml/14 fl oz/2 cups water in a saucepan. Bring to the boil. Reduce the heat to medium-low, close the lid and cook for 30 minutes.

2 While the meat is cooking, heat the ghee or oil in a heavy-bottomed saucepan on medium heat.

3 Add the onion seeds and brown them for 5 seconds.

4 Put in the sesame seeds and then the bay leaves, garlic, ginger and onions and fry them until golden brown.

5 Add the cooked meat pieces to the saucepan and cook until all the liquid has been absorbed.

6 Stir in the ground almonds, coriander, roasted cumin, garam masala, red chilli, turmeric, mace, nutmeg and salt. Turn the heat off and set to one side, ensuring all the meat is cooked.

7 Pour in 50 ml/2 fl oz/3½ tbsp water and cook again until all the water is absorbed and the ghee/oil appears on the surface of the mixture.

8 Repeat this 2 or 3 times. Adding only small quantities of water will not only help to fry nicely but will also stop the spitting and splashing.

9 When the meat is tender, turn the heat off, sprinkle over the garnish before serving.

SERVING SUGGESTION:

Serve hot with puri, dal, rayta and an egg curry or apple curry dish.

BHARWA TOMATAR

STUFFED TOMATOES

SERVES: 4–6

S tuffed tomatoes make a very attractive party side dish. For this dish one needs firm tomatoes of equal size.

INGREDIENTS:	METRIC	IMPERIAL	AMERICAN
Firm tomatoes	*500 g*	*1 lb 2 oz*	*4$\frac{1}{2}$ cups*
Oil	*75 ml*	*5 tbsp*	*5 tbsp*
Mustard seeds	*5 ml*	*1 tsp*	*1 tsp*
Potatoes, boiled in jackets, peeled and cut into tiny pieces	*500 g*	*1 lb 2 oz*	*4$\frac{1}{2}$ cups*
Garam masala	*5 ml*	*1 tsp*	*1 tsp*
Ground coriander/cilantro	*5 ml*	*1 tsp*	*1 tsp*
Ground roasted cumin	*5 ml*	*1 tsp*	*1 tsp*
Ground red chilli	*2.5 ml*	*$\frac{1}{2}$ tsp*	*$\frac{1}{2}$ tsp*
Ground turmeric	*2.5 ml*	*$\frac{1}{2}$ tsp*	*$\frac{1}{2}$ tsp*
Salt to taste			
Mixed vegetables, frozen or fresh (ready-cooked)	*250 g*	*9 oz*	*2$\frac{1}{4}$ cups*
Raisins	*100 g*	*4 oz*	*$\frac{1}{2}$ cup*
Green coriander/cilantro leaves, chopped	*30 ml*	*2 tbsp*	*2 tbsp*
Small green chilli	*1*	*1*	*1*
Oil for frying			

COOKING TIME: 25 MINUTES

1 Slice about 3 mm/⅛ in off the top of the tomatoes and skin them. Scoop out the pulp and reserve.

2 Heat the oil in a flat frying pan (skillet) on medium heat. Add the mustard seeds and when they start crackling fry the potato pieces on a medium-low heat for 5 minutes or until they are light golden brown.

STEP 21

3 Stir in the garam masala, coriander, roasted cumin, red chilli, turmeric, salt and then the mixed vegetables and the tomato pulp and cook for 7 minutes.

4 Put in the raisins and stir well. Mix in the chopped coriander leaves and green chilli and turn the heat off.

5 Stuff the tomatoes with the potato mixture. Replace the tops.

6 Heat 45 ml/3 tbsp oil in a frying pan (skillet) on a medium-low heat. Place all the stuffed tomatoes in the frying pan and fry them for 2 minutes. Gently turn them over and fry for a further minute. Alternatively, put the tomatoes in a greased tray, sprinkled with oil and bake in a preheated oven at 200°C/400°F/gas mark 6 for 10 minutes.

GARNISH SUGGESTION:

Place one cooked tomato in the centre of the serving dish and arrange the rest of the tomatoes around it in a circle. Spread the leftover filling around the tomatoes.

SERVING SUGGESTION:

Serve hot with chutney, pulao, puri, dal, yoghurt and a chicken dish.

KHOYA KI SABJI

PUNJABI STYLE VEGETARIAN KEEMA

SERVES:

This exquisite dish is served during parties. The combination of khoya, nuts and sauce produces a lovely flavour.

INGREDIENTS:	METRIC	IMPERIAL	AMERICAN
Ghee	60 ml	4 tbsp	4 tbsp
Large garlic cloves, crushed	1	1	1
Fresh ginger, finely chopped	1.2 cm	$1/2$ in	$1/2$ in
Medium onion, finely chopped	1	1	1
Bay leaves	2	2	2
Garam masala	5 ml	1 tsp	1 tsp
Ground roasted cumin	5 ml	1 tsp	1 tsp
Ground coriander/cilantro	5 ml	1 tsp	1 tsp
Ground red chilli	2.5 ml	$1/2$ tsp	$1/2$ tsp
Ground turmeric	1.5 ml	$1/4$ tsp	$1/4$ tsp
Salt to taste			
Mixed vegetables, cooked	150 g	5 oz	1 cup
Tomatoes, tinned	230 g	8 oz	1 cup
Khoya (see page 25), broken in large lumps	150 g	5 oz	$2/3$ cup
Raisins	100 g	4 oz	$2/3$ cup
Cashew-nuts, cut into halves lengthwise	50 g	2 oz	$1/2$ cup
Ground green cardamom	2.5 ml	$1/2$ tsp	$1/2$ tsp

TO GARNISH:

Garam masala	1.5 ml	$1/4$ tsp	$1/4$ tsp
Green coriander/cilantro leaves, chopped	15 ml	1 tbsp	1 tbsp
Small green chilli, chopped			

COOKING TIME: 20 MINUTES

1 Heat the ghee in a large heavy-bottomed saucepan on a medium heat.

2 Add the garlic, ginger, onion and the bay leaves and fry until golden brown.

3 Stir in the spices, salt, mixed vegetables and then the tomatoes and fry until all the liquid has been absorbed and the ghee appears on the surface of the mixture.

4 Mix in the khoya, raisins and nuts, reduce the heat to low and cook for a further 2 minutes.

5 Sprinkle over the garnish before serving.

SERVING SUGGESTION:

Serve hot with puri, pulao, rayta and a pumpkin kofta dish.

VEGETABLE BIRYANI

SERVES: 4–6

Due to my experimental nature with food this delightful dish came into existence. Yellow corn with paneer in a dark coloured sauce and layers of nutty saffron rice makes it very attractive. Its aroma increases the appetite.

PREPARING THE VEGETABLE LAYER:

INGREDIENTS:	METRIC	IMPERIAL	AMERICAN
Oil or ghee	60 ml	4 tbsp	4 tbsp
Cumin seeds	2.5 ml	$^1\!/_2$ tsp	$^1\!/_2$ tsp
Large garlic cloves, crushed	2	2	2
Fresh ginger, finely chopped	1.2 cm	$^1\!/_2$ in	$^1\!/_2$ in
Medium onion, finely chopped	1	1	1
Coconut, desiccated, or fresh, grated	60 ml	4 tbsp	4 tbsp
Garam masala	5 ml	1 tsp	1 tsp
Ground coriander/cilantro	5 ml	1 tsp	1 tsp
Ground roasted cumin	5 ml	1 tsp	1 tsp
Ground red chilli	2.5 ml	$^1\!/_2$ tsp	$^1\!/_2$ tsp
Ground turmeric	2.5 ml	$^1\!/_2$ tsp	$^1\!/_2$ tsp
Salt to taste			
Tomatoes, tinned	400 g	14 oz	$1^3\!/_4$ cups
Sweetcorn/corn, frozen, loose (or any other vegetable)	250 g	9 oz	$2^1\!/_4$ cups
Paneer (see page 23) cut into 1.2 cm/$^1\!/_2$ in square pieces	1.2 litres	2 pts	5 cups
Green coriander/cilantro leaves, chopped	2	2	2
Lemon juice	30 ml	2 tbsp	2 tbsp
Mint leaves, chopped	15 ml	1 tbsp	1 tbsp

COOKING TIME: 25 MINUTES

1 Heat the oil or ghee in a heavy-bottomed large saucepan on medium heat and brown the cumin seeds.

2 Add the garlic, ginger and onion and fry until golden brown.

3 Put in the coconut and fry for a further 2 minutes.

4 Stir in the garam masala, coriander, cumin, red chilli, turmeric, salt and then the tomatoes, corn and the paneer. Cook until all the liquid has been absorbed.

5 Mix in the coriander, lemon juice and mint leaves thoroughly. Set the pan on one side (reheat before placing in layers with the rice). Prepare the rice while the corn is cooking.

PREPARING THE RICE LAYER:

Ghee	90 ml	6 tbsp	6 tbsp
Cumin seeds	5 ml	1 tsp	1 tsp
Medium onion, thinly sliced	1	1	1
*Cloves	4	4	4
*Peppercorns	4	4	4
*Black cardamom	1	1	1
*Cinnamon stick	2.5 cm	1 in	1 in
*Bay leaves	2	2	2
Rice (patna or basmati), cleaned, washed and drained	250 g	9 oz	1¼ cups
Garam masala	5 ml	1 tsp	1 tsp
Ground roasted cumin	5 ml	1 tsp	1 tsp
Salt to taste			
Raisins	100 g	4 oz	⅔ cup
Cashew-nuts, cut in halves lengthwise	50 g	2 oz	½ cup
Water	500 ml	20 fl oz	2½ cups

COOKING TIME: 20 MINUTES

1 Heat the ghee in a large heavy-bottomed saucepan and brown the cumin seeds.

2 Add the onion, cloves, peppercorns, black cardamom, bay leaves and cinnamon and fry until golden brown.

3 Mix in the rice and fry for 2 minutes.

4 Stir in the garam masala, cumin, salt and then the raisins, cashew-nuts and the water.

5 Bring to the boil, reduce the heat to low, close the lid and cook for 15 minutes.

LAYERING THE RICE AND THE VEGETABLES:

Milk, warm	50 ml	2 fl oz	3½ tbsp
Saffron	2.5 ml	½ tsp	½ tsp

1 Place the saffron in the warm milk.

2 Take a heavy-bottomed saucepan and fill it with alternate layers of vegetables and rice. Repeat until you have used all the mixture.

3 Pour the saffron milk over the vegetables and layers of rice.

4 Close the lid and cook on a low heat for a further 5 minutes.

5 To serve, place a serving dish on the saucepan and carefully turn over. Tap a little all over the saucepan with a spoon.

6 Gently lift the saucepan, making sure all the biryani is in the serving dish.

SERVING SUGGESTION:

Serve hot with rayta, salad and carrot matar.

RASGULLA

MAKES: 10

Rasgulla is a famous and delicious sweet dish from the Bengal. It is white coloured, light, soft and juicy, made from paneer (Indian style cheese). Bengali sweets are very popular all over India.

INGREDIENTS:	METRIC	IMPERIAL	AMERICAN
Milk	1.2 litres	2 pts	5 cups
Lemon juice	45 ml	3 tbsp	3 tbsp

1 Heat the milk and just as it begins to boil add the lemon juice (to separate the milk). Turn the heat off and leave for 2 minutes.

2 Strain the curd from the whey using a muslin cloth (keeping the whey for cooking lentils or vegetables).

3 Wash the curd (paneer) with cold water to remove any remaining fat from it.

4 Squeeze out all the water and press under a heavy object (a large saucepan filled with water) on top of an upturned plate for 30 minutes.

Water	2.5 litres	4 pts	10 cups
Sugar	350 g	12 oz	1½ cups
Semolina	10 ml	2 tsp	2 tsp
Essence: gulab or kevera water	5 ml	1 tsp	1 tsp

COOKING TIME: 1 HOUR AND 20 MINUTES

1 Place the water and sugar in a large saucepan for boiling on medium heat (if you do not have a large saucepan, boil the sugar in less water and add boiling water to the pan as needed until you have made up to the required amount).

2 While the syrup is boiling, mix the paneer and the semolina in a bowl with the palm of your hand until it is soft and springy.

3 Divide into about 10 equal portions and in the palms of your hands roll into tight balls. Add the paneer balls to the boiling syrup and cook for 1 hour and until the syrup is reduced to a quarter of the volume.

4 Remove from the heat and cool. When very cold put it in a bowl with the syrup. Keep it in a refrigerator for 3–4 hours before serving.

5 Stir in the essence just before serving.

SERVING SUGGESTION:

Serve cold at tea with samosa and pakora or after the meal as a dessert.

INDEX